Parentonomics

Parentonomics

An Economist Dad Looks at Parenting

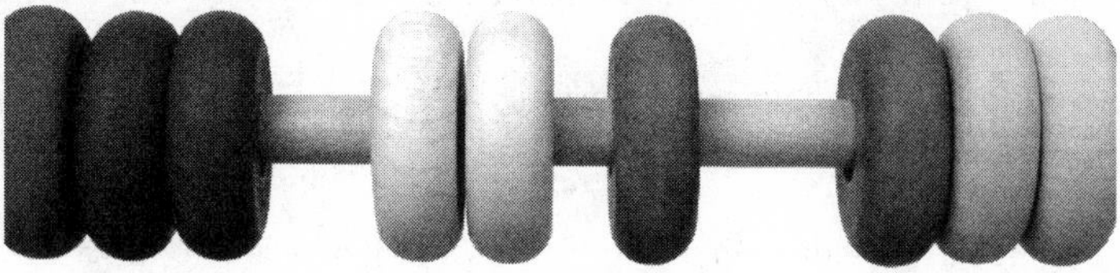

Joshua Gans

The MIT Press
Cambridge, Massachusetts
London, England

For information about special quantity discounts, please e-mail special_sales@mitpress.mit.edu

This book was set in Sabon and Helvetica round by SNP Best-set Typesetter Ltd., Hong Kong.
Printed and bound in the United States of America.

Library of Congress Cataloging-in-Publication Data
Gans, Joshua, 1968–
Parentonomics : an economist dad looks at parenting / Joshua Gans.
p. cm.
Includes bibliographical references and index.
ISBN 978-0-262-01278-2 (hardcover : alk. paper)
1. Parenting. 2. Child rearing—Economic aspects.
3. Responsibility in children. I. Title.
HQ769.G257 2009
332.024′0085—dc22

2008032752

10 9 8 7 6 5 4 3 2 1

Published for sale in Australia and New Zealand by University of New South Wales Press Ltd.

To N, B, A, and the other A.
They are this book.

Contents

Preface

One of the most challenging parts of lecturing in economics is making it relevant for students. My strategy has been to liberally use examples from popular culture to bring ideas into the classroom. Thinking about how Monica and Rachel from *Friends* could divide up household chores, what sustained the reputation of the Dread Pirate Roberts in *The Princess Bride,* and the protocols for haggling in *The Life of Brian* could easily fill up an undergraduate classroom. But when it came to teaching MBAs, there was a new challenge. Their ages and age range made it hard to find the salient pop culture references. And their craving for relevance to their own careers and decisions drove everything. Sure, I could find examples from business—but usually they were so bound up with complexity and context that it was hard to make them hit home in one crisp, clear blow.

Then, in 1998, we had our first child. All of a sudden our everyday life became one big economic management problem. Not every parent sees it this way, but every parent faces the same issues. Among the more mature students in my classroom there was both empathy and common ground. And so, slowly at first, as I gathered my own experiences, I began using parenting examples to illustrate economic points.

A lot of my classes involved predicting what might happen if you introduce change when two or more people interact with one another; something that happens in markets and inside firms every day. One such situation is where a person—termed, in economics, the principal—is trying to get another—the agent—to do something they ordinarily would not want to do; like an employer trying to get an employee to work hard. Suffice it to say, this situation alone describes the life of a parent. You, the principal, try to get your child, the agent, to do various things, from sleeping, eating, toileting, and behaving to refraining from lying, cheating, stealing, and the use of violence on others. The question was whether economics—which worries a lot about incentives—could be of any use to parents—who also worry a lot about incentives.

It is perhaps a misconception among noneconomists that economists are unduly enamored by incentives and what they might do for the world. Indeed, nothing could be further from the truth. Yes, it is true that incentives appropriately applied, in an appropriate situation, can generate some good outcomes. But, more often than not, putting incentives in place is risky. Much can go wrong. For instance, if you make an employee's pay depend upon their sales outcomes, you can find yourself losing those employees in recessions or end up having to pay them more, on average, to compensate. Or, if you give an employee a bonus for outperforming their sales numbers this year compared with last year, don't be surprised if they shift their numbers and maybe client deliveries around to make sure there is always growth.

As I tried to illustrate the ways that incentives could go wrong, my own parenting experiences increasingly came to the fore. And while it was not all I talked about, it is what students appeared to remember. When I saw them years later, they would recount back to me the story of how my daughter, who was allowed a treat if she successfully went to the toilet, would sit there until something came out. They would tell me that it actually changed the way they approached a contract negotiation or a personnel management issue. It wasn't that they were treating the other side like children, just that the story had made the economic message stick.

And they were not the only ones. My colleagues, in particular, seemed to enjoy the economic content in my own parenting dilemmas. They weren't learning from it as much as laughing at my struggles, feeling empathy, or using it as an opportunity to amuse themselves about how economists survive in the real world. A fellow economist and good friend, Catherine de Fontenay, urged me to start writing this stuff down. It took a while, but I finally accepted that advice and started a blog.[1] As a new year's resolution to write about economics and parenting, I wrote one long post on January 2, 2003. However, as is the nature of these things, there it remained until 2006 when I took up blogging in earnest and rediscovered it. A few months later, it seemed that there might be enough material for a book. Those who had initially urged me to write, now urged me to reach beyond the blog. And so *Parentonomics* was born.

Nonetheless, a few disclaimers are in order. In my day job, I'm an economics professor. That means a few things. One is that I generally write about things that I have researched and can claim some expertise about. This book, however, is far from scholarly. While I can claim expertise in the economics you will read about in the ensuing pages, the parenting is another matter.

I have never researched parenting science and child behavior beyond my reading as a layperson. There is a lot of research out there in psychology and related disciplines, but it is beyond my expertise to digest it and offer authoritative commentary on it. Many of the ideas I put forward here may not be original, so I don't want to claim them as such.

What's more, my parenting experience could hardly be claimed to be the norm. I have three children, and so the experiences I recount here are based at best on that sample of three. This is not the sort of experience you would use to tell you something about averages or anything scientific.

Instead, my goals are much more limited. This book continues my mission to educate the world about economics and what it can do. I will illustrate various economic concepts, but only as they relate to parenting issues.[2] This means that my coverage of economics will be haphazard and incomplete. Despite this, my modest hope is that in reading this book, you will learn a bit more about economics and economists—and about their limitations. I'd like to think that my own trials might even entertain you along the way.

I want to be able to look back upon this book as a record of what I was thinking during a particularly important period of my life. It is very personal. As you read it, you'll learn a lot about my children and my spouse, and about me. Occasionally, you will learn about my friends, and some others who have put their stories in the public domain. You'll find that I have a distinctively economic perspective on things, and you might find that somewhat stark.

This book should not be considered a parenting manual. I will offer advice. I find it hard not to. But, as a scholar, I want to warn you to discount this as anything prescriptive—you'll need to make your own parenting choices.

Nonetheless, as with all such books, this one may provoke you to think more about choices you face or will face as a parent. What I offer is a fresh perspective, a way of looking at parenting issues that is different, analytical, and maybe even useful; or at the very least, amusing. I know that I enjoy reading what anyone says about child rearing. So it may be that this book adds to the mix, stirring up its own juice and bringing out some flavor.

Acknowledgments

I didn't write this book alone. As I already mentioned, I need to thank my colleague, Catherine de Fontenay, who was instrumental in getting me to see that my experiences might be worth taking to a wider audience. Thanks also to my longstanding coauthor, Andrew Leigh, who stimulated my interest in blogging as well as in various issues to do with birth timing that became the very first chapter here. And on that score, I have to thank numerous academics, family, and friends who have read and contributed to various parts of the book: Terri Apter, Susan Athey, Mark Crosby, Cathy Fazio, Jeremy Gans, Shane Greenstein, Stephen King, Barry Nalebuff, Christine Neill, Heather Schultz, Richard Speed, and Scott Stern. My own experiences would not have been nearly rich enough to carry the day alone.

I would also like to add my thanks to some predecessors who cleared the path for my work here. *Cheaper by the Dozen* did for parenting and time management what I am hoping to do here for economics. Emily Bazelon's irregular columns in *Slate* stimulated many a blog post. And Tyler Cowen, Stephen

Dubner, Ross Gittins, Greg Mankiw, Tim Harford, Paul Krugman, Steve Landsburg, Steve Levitt, and John Quiggin have similarly done economists a great service by opening up the field to popular writing through books and blogs.

Special thanks also to my sister-in-law, Michelle Lippey, who found me the publisher of the book, and to the team at New South and at the MIT Press.

Finally, I thank my unnamed spouse (N) (who dutifully read the chapters here and whose laughter determined what stayed in and what went out) and my three wonderful and also unnamed children—Children No. 1, No. 2, and No. 3. You are anonymous to protect the innocent. But if you weren't who you are, this book wouldn't be what it is, and I would not be anything like the person I am. There is no way I can express in words the magnitude of my debt to you all for giving me my life. Although I guess a fat royalty check won't go astray.

PART I

THE BEGINNING

1 Planning

It was a month before the due date of Child No. 1 when our obstetrician forecast that our baby was going to be large; definitely over eight pounds. Now that wasn't truly abnormal. To get CNN coverage, you need a child to kick in above thirteen pounds. But our prognosis was enough to start a discussion about options. In our case, this was whether to have the baby induced; a noninvasive procedure by which chemicals are used to start childbirth.

Child No. 1's mother-to-be was instantly attracted to the idea. Basically, any option that reduced the number of days or minutes of pregnancy was appealing at this point. I too was happy to get on with it, but only after making a show of the "so long as it is in the interests of the child" argument. Nonetheless, we were assured that all this was pretty normal fare. And in the ensuing weeks, the size issue became more certain and the back pain more extreme, so our delivery was scheduled to begin at 8 a.m. on a Sunday morning, a week or so before the due date.

Let's skip forward about two years. Child No. 2's due date was just before Christmas. This time, the timing discussion occurred many months before—I think around August. We were told that, of course, we wouldn't want to be in the hospital around Christmas. And being self-interested Jews, pleased with our first planned delivery, we promptly agreed. So the birth was booked for another Sunday morning, well over a week before December 25. Presumably, this allowed our obstetrician to engage in some scheduling too.

Our experience has two features—one uncommon and the other quite common. First, the uncommon. When it comes to scheduled deliveries—whether inductions or planned cesareans—these are usually put on weekdays and not weekends. Indeed, as these procedures have become more commonplace around the world, the share of weekend births has dropped off considerably. These days 30 percent fewer babies are born on any given Saturday or Sunday compared with a weekday. But we had not one but two planned weekend births; quite a rarity.

Now to the common. It turns out that, in Australia, there is a spike in births every year around mid-December. Birth counts tend downward from about October, then blip upward in mid-December before falling to a low point on Christmas Day. The story here is easy to imagine, and the chances are that both doctors and patients have an interest in getting things out the way early.

But other trends in birth timing are more one-sided. Some of the most technical of economic theories suggest that when people are almost indifferent about something, little things can tip the balance. So it is when it comes to birth timing. Generally, people wouldn't care much whether a baby is born on a Tuesday, Wednesday, or Thursday. But if that Wednesday is April 1 or February 29 (should it occur), then they would prefer their child's birthday to be on the Tuesday or Thursday.

Indeed, on inauspicious days, the birth rate falls by 11 to 16 percent. So just to avoid some potential embarrassment over birthday parties, parents will pressure their doctors and succeed in having the births moved a day or so.[1]

This is all very well, but what happens if the parental and obstetric preferences collide? This brings me back to the whole business of weekends. It is easy to imagine why obstetricians and maternity hospitals might like to reduce the birth rate then. Having time off on weekends is valuable and possibly cost-effective. But some have argued that this is what parents prefer too. In my mind, it is harder to make the case that, on average, parents might care one way or the other.

They *might* care if, say, April 1 fell on a Friday or a Monday. Then they may want to schedule a birth for the weekend, while an obstetrician would want to avoid it. The result would likely be some traditional haggling, but presumably without any money changing hands.

By comparing the April Fool's Day effect for Fridays and Mondays with the same effect for other days (both weekday and weekend where there are no conflicts), we can tease out what happens. In Australia, it appears that the obstetrician wins about three-quarters of the time.[2] So, when there is a conflict, the doctor holds the upper hand. Parents can push these things around, but only so much. Scheduling is going to largely fit the doctor's interests.[3]

But what happens when money is added to the mix? It doesn't happen often, but the evidence suggests that when it is, it plays a big role.

For example, in the United States the tax system gives parents an incentive to bring births back from the new tax year into the old, through a combination of a child tax credit and the earned-income credit. Stacey Dickert-Conlin and Amitabh Chandra discovered that, on average, an increased tax benefit of just $500 raised the probability of a birth in the last week of December by 26.9 percent.[4] This is despite the fact that in other countries, births around that time of year are scheduled before or after that week.

These days the tax benefit is larger (around $3,300), and so it is likely that thousands of babies, who otherwise would be born in the first week of January, arrive a week earlier. So rather than September (otherwise the most popular month), December 28 has become the big birth day. Not surprisingly, this poses an annual scheduling issue for maternity wards and is a source of competition for places among parents.[5]

But at least, when these things occur annually, scheduling is possible. In Australia, fiddling with government policy led to a big birthday surprise on July 1, 2004. That day recorded the most births in Australian history.

To explain why, I need to take you back to the evening of May 11, 2004. That day was budget night; a night when the

Australian government announces its broad tax and spending policies for the coming year. Suffice it to say, it is not the most interesting event on the calendar, but given that I was in the business, I watched the speech.

On that night, something grabbed my attention:

> The Government will roll together the existing Maternity Allowance and the Baby Bonus into a new payment, a Maternity Payment, to be paid to all mothers on the birth of a child. The payment will be a lump sum of $3000 from 1 July and will rise to $5000 by 1 July 2008. Those who are receiving the current Baby Bonus will keep that entitlement where it is higher than this. The Maternity Payment recognizes the cost of a new child and will assist all mothers, many of whom leave the workforce and leave paid work at the time of the birth of their child.

Now you could be forgiven for missing it in the raft of terminology, but this was a significant announcement. For starters, I found out that there was an existing incentive payment for having babies that I was unaware of; as it turns out, it was directed at lower-income folk. That payment would disappear in favor of cold hard cash: three thousand Australian dollars. No income test, no taxation, just a straight-out payment. Produce a child and you get the cash.

Normally, that wouldn't be enough to get me excited. But on that day, "we" were seven months pregnant with Child No. 3. So I was quite thrilled to learn that it was likely that, next year, I would be watching the budget speech on a plasma screen TV. A few seconds later, I ran to check on what the due date of our baby was. By the time you get to a third child, you don't have all the details at your fingertips. I had a vague notion of July; but was it early July?

Our expected due date was in late July. Phew! That gave us lots of room. Nonetheless, Child No. 3's mother was unimpressed when I strongly suggested that we make sure we reach July; we could think delaying thoughts if necessary. As with Children Nos. 1 and 2, her preference continued to be the sooner the better. But one could hope.

Following blatant self-interest, the economist side of me started to take over. I came to a simple but definite prediction: "There aren't going to be any babies born on June 30, 2004." My reason for that was purely economic. I figured that it wouldn't be too hard to alter birth certificates and the like, and that that's what would happen. Pretty cynical, I know, but I am an economist; we are paid to think like that. But it was more than that. Given certain observed preferences for shorter pregnancies, it seemed likely that "fiddling the books" was the main thing that might happen as a result of all of this. Was it worth any money to delay a real birth?

As July 1 came closer, reports came in that parents were delaying births to get the bonus. It was put to the government that perhaps it would have been better to have introduced the policy right back in May when it was announced. But the health minister, Kay Patterson, was unconcerned, "Well if I thought that mothers would put their babies at risk, but I don't believe mothers would put them at risk."[6]

Usually, governments try to avoid giving people big incentives for fraud or to affect medical decisions. This time the Australian government—admittedly to save $100 million in payouts—had done the opposite. The question was, what would the data show?

The data spoke for itself, with a seismic disruption around June 30—a big drop in births, followed by the inevitable rise. What's more, it turns out that July 1, 2004, had the most births in a single day over the thirty years of recorded birth data in Australia. The second of July was no slouch either, being the seventh highest day. This was a big effect. Over a thousand births across the country were shifted, ostensibly due to the new Baby Bonus being introduced.[7]

Was it "fiddling the books"? If it was, it wouldn't be a big worry, because nothing real was actually affected. If you have a government handout like this, who cares if a few extra people get it? But it doesn't look like fiddling was what happened.

Instead, births themselves were shifted, which is much more worrying. We know this because, first, when we look at the types of procedures, it was all in inducements and cesareans. "Normal" deliveries were unaffected, which would not be the case if books were fiddled. Second, June was an unusually low month for births, and July (as a whole) was an unusually high month. Indeed, one quarter of all births were shifted by more than two weeks!

When we arrived at the hospital in late July for Child No. 3, it was still crowded; the nursing staff told us it had been a very busy month. They were using the overflow wing, and the usual eagerness to schedule an inducement for us had been absent (Child No. 3 arrived naturally early on a Sunday morning). This means that our birth day was disrupted because of the major disruption earlier in the month. This was a considerable effect.

Maternity hospitals are a nice planned business. They know who is coming and approximately when. Even though there are some tax issues in the United States, they are still able to plan. Such hospitals don't have to deal with epidemics and accidents. To face such a major disruption across the whole country is worrying. Were staffing levels appropriate? When you look at more detailed data, there are no immediate signs of health issues; but babies were, on average, bigger than usual. That is what happens if you leave things in the oven longer.

And you might think that all this birth date adjustment was brought about by poorer families in society. But that doesn't appear to be the case. It seems that the biggest shifts were made for parents who lived in areas with higher incomes. Why might this be so? Well, it comes back down to bargaining. In Australia, we have a dual-level health care system, consisting of a freely provided public system and a paid-for private one (mostly used by higher-income people). My best guess is that private providers were able to find ways to accommodate parents who wanted to delay births, something not open to public patients.

The moral of all of this is that it's amazing what people will do for even a relatively small financial reward. I, for one, am happy we didn't really have to think about that. And I'm enjoying the new television.[8]

2 Delivering

One of the big ideas in economics is that togetherness is good. Rather than try to do everything ourselves, we should share the load. It saves time, giving us the chance to spend more time on things we are really good at. This thought preoccupied me as I sat through six long hours of childbirth classes.

Birthing classes have two purposes. The first is to inform. Within months, a big event is going to occur. And you only have to look around the room to get the sense of foreboding that accompanies a ticking time bomb. So it might help if you became more aware of the gruesome details of it all.

The second purpose, as I see it, is to try and work out what the half of the class who aren't pregnant are going to do on the Big Day. That issue gave rise to two reactions from the pregnant half of our class. The first was, "Hasn't he done enough already? 'Doing' is how we got into this mess. Perhaps give him a computer game to play with or a TV to watch and otherwise leave me alone."

Now this reaction should be given its due. Indeed, for the greater part of human history, the expectation was that Daddy should wait outside. My dad did this. He went to the hospital prepared with a magazine and a pen and somehow lost both. The only thing he was expected to do was keep out of the way. What is more, the hospitals preferred it this way and restricted fathers-to-be to the waiting room.

But times have changed. There was a call for men to become more involved. At first, it was all done in secret. Midwives would hide men away in closets. Then it became the norm and the expectation. Hospital policy changed, and birthing classes immersed themselves in the issue, but many who were pregnant still held the view: "Like he could help!" Times change, but reactions don't necessarily come along for the ride.

This brings me to the other reaction. It was along the lines of, "Yes! How can we make sure *he* shares *my* pain?'

Now to an economist, this is a perfectly reasonable reaction. Remember, we should share the load. So I was all for this. Put me in a closet, or whatever you like. I was there to help. The obvious problem was: how, exactly? Apparently, it was the job of birthing classes to work that out.

One possible pain-sharing solution would of course be for Daddy to literally share Mommy's pain. Comedic writer Dave Barry (who we will come back to in a minute) puts it thus:

> My wife thinks the only fair system would be if, every time the woman had a contraction, she got to hit her husband on the body part of her choice with a ball-peen hammer. Of course, she is kidding. But only because her contractions have not yet started.[1]

Now I should point out that, strictly speaking, the total amount of pain going around would go up with this solution. (I have no idea what a "ball-peen hammer" is, but it sounds nasty.) At least, in this scenario, the experience of pain would be shared.

This might strike you as a potentially inefficient state of affairs. But it could have an economic rationale. After all, if it gave Mommy comfort to see Daddy suffer through this, then one can't complain that there are no winners. The principle of "equality of suffering" can soften a load. And if Mommy feels better, then we can say that something has been shared.

It appears that this isn't really what people have in mind with regard to pain sharing. The midwives in our birthing class expressed with glee another way this was done: by embarrassing Daddy.

Their experience told them that, during the last stages of delivery, more than just the baby comes out. That is when Mommy lets rip at Daddy and airs, in public, all of his dirty laundry. What is more, given the situation, Daddy can't respond and has to just take it with a pained smile.

This appeared to be a big job perk for the midwives, and they looked around the room at each of us, trying to forecast who was likely to provide the best entertainment. I imagine a scramble for the roster would then be on. In our class, it was clear that some of the nonpregnant had cause to be worried.

But again, this method seems like it would simply create more pain, in the sense that some daddies would feel the pain of embarrassment, but no real comfort would be given to mommies. Or perhaps letting loose would be just what the doctor ordered.

The more "constructive" segments of the class focused on various forms of pain management. These can be neatly divided into two categories: those that involved drugs, and those that didn't.

Now our instructors wanted to extol the virtues of the drug-free options. This is where Daddy could put in some effort to assist in reducing pain. But ultimately, I had a sense that the suggestions were misguided.

Apparently, the big thing that Daddy could do was provide several hours of relaxing massage. Much time was spent on describing how this could be done, given that the massagee would be in labor.

At first I listened intently, but then something dawned on me. When we are on vacation, Mommy-to-be pays for a professional massage. And at that time, there is no immediate therapeutic benefit; certainly not in the extreme way she was about to experience. So why, on delivery day, is this something for *me* to handle? Let's face it, I may be lots of things, but expert masseuse is not one of them.

So if a massage was going to be critical, we should call in a professional. Indeed, shouldn't the hospital have some sort of service? Think about what we would be willing to pay! But there was no mention of this.

There was only one conclusion I could draw: they were just trying to find something for Daddy to do. Something that would seem useful, but would be dispensed with in minutes at the request of Mommy. Massages are not actually what those in labor want or need at the time.

If we are going to find a role for Daddy in helping with the pain, we were going to have to find something that (a) would work and (b) he could do. And that was going to depend upon the couple.

When I put my mind to this, I came up with a solution: I was going to read Dave Barry to her. While the previous quote from him might suggest otherwise, Dave Barry writes mostly about other things,[2] and on delivery days, we left the birthing stories behind. It was more than enough to leave us convulsed in laughter, tears running down our faces, and every few minutes someone would pop their head into the room, wondering if we were all right. They had never seen a couple in that situation have so much fun. But eventually we had to calm down. The laughs were interfering with the contraction-measuring machine.

Actually, that machine—which I lovingly called the "contraction-meter"—kept me amused and interested through the many hours of labor. I would sit next to it and watch the printed readout. Most of the time nothing much happened. Then suddenly a seismic event would register. I would remark, "Ooh, that was a big one. Did you feel that?" A whimpered reply would follow. I may have not been feeling her pain, but I was at least on top of the statistics.

Which brings me to drugs. This is the stuff that actually *can* remove the pain. Childbirth classes talk a lot about options, from gas to a needle in the spine. For the pregnant ones, gas is an immediate sell. An epidural or needle option is, at that time, a last resort. But as Dave Barry would say, "That is only because her contractions haven't started."

With regard to drugs, it therefore falls on Daddy to understand the options and to enact the wishes of Mommy, presuming that she was actually sane. It is put to us that, at some point on delivery day, she will go insane and start demanding narcotics. Daddy's job is to make sure they have discussed the appropriate response beforehand and to implement her wishes at the time. He must treat the decision to use drugs with the solemnity of a decision, say, to put down one's pet dog.

That, as they say, is easier said than done. Daddy is very quickly turned from the voice of reason to drug pimp. When that moment comes, he is actually responsible for ensuring that hospital staff act quickly and do whatever it takes to stop the pain. He needs to be seen to shout, bribe, and, if necessary, use force to ensure drugs are administered.

We did that about nine hours into the (induced) labor of Child No. 1, long after the Dave Barry had worn off. An anesthetist came by, and Mommy happily submitted to what seemed to me to be spinal surgery. She then fell asleep, leaving me to enjoy dinner in peace. I came away from that experience thinking that no time was too soon for drugs in labor. Perhaps at the onset of pregnancy.

It turns out, however, that that is not true, as we found out with Child No. 2. Our drug request duly went in and was administered early. Then, well before the baby was out, the drug wore off. By that time there was no chance of another dose. This was the first time Mommy actually felt raw childbirth. And it wasn't pretty. You see, all of our babies were born posterior. What that means is that instead of coming out face down, they came out face up. For mother and baby, this means that their spines rub together like jagged tectonic plates. And if you squirm at that thought, then I have shared some more pain!

It was at this point that the truth came out. Not, as the midwives were hoping, about me. Instead, it was the truth about my real usefulness in their eyes. It's as if we were back in the 1950s. They decided that I wasn't—and could not be—useful. It turns out that, on this occasion, they were mistaken.

Child No. 2's mother needed comforting to get through this. The midwives tried to provide this in a "supportive" manner. It didn't suit her, and she screamed at them to "shut the f**k up," but not so politely. They would tell her how well she was doing and that it would all be over soon. They would wipe her brow with a damp cloth. And she hated them for it. To this day, she still remembers her annoyance at the water trickling down her neck.

It was at this point that I took over the comforting function. It was, believe it or not, something I knew how to do. So I started cracking jokes, trying to be as Dave Barry-like as possible. The key was distraction.

I remember distinctly providing support on one leg while the obstetrician was on the other. I started asking him trivia questions. "So what's the most number of deliveries you have had in a single day?" (five it turns out) "What's your largest baby?" "Have you ever delivered conjoined twins?" And so on. Fortunately, he was into it, but the midwives were not.

They were horrified. They could not believe how unsupportive I was. Indeed, three-and-a-half years later, we would arrive at the same maternity ward for Child No. 3. A midwife would come into our room, and I would be politely introduced, "This is my husband, Joshua."

"Oh, yes, we know him," was the contemptuous reply. It must have been thousands of babies later, and I was still infamous, my picture adorning their coffeeroom wall or dart board.

But to this day, Child No. 2's mother remembers all my jokes and the trivia, and it did take her mind off things. They didn't teach me that in childbirth class, but when it came down to it, I knew her better than anyone else. At last, there was something I was useful for.

The drug issue all came to a head with Child No. 3. She was our noninduced baby, and the one where we had the 2 a.m. hospital rush. We got there, and labor was on. True to form we immediately had a discussion with the midwife about drugs.

I listened quietly as the midwife tried to convince Child No. 3's mother that perhaps we should wait and see. The fact that the previous two births were posterior was raised, but it wasn't certain that was the case now. Eventually, as she was leaning toward waiting, Child No. 3's mother turned to me and asked: "What do you think?"

Without hesitation I said unequivocally, "I think you are broadly delusional. You need drugs and you need them now."

The midwife looked at me, her eyes burning with the intensity of what felt like a thousand suns. I was living up to my reputation there. And, what is more, my advice was not heeded.

An hour later, insanity had set in, and Child No. 3's mother demanded drugs. She was examined and then told it was too late. The cervix was too far dilated. She would have to go drug free. She turned to me and said, "You're going to tell me I told you so, aren't you?" I said, "No, it will be all right." (Clearly, I left that until I could get it into print here.) Then I lied through my teeth and told her this would all be best for the baby. She didn't really believe me but appreciated my effort to cloud the truth.

A final role was revealed for Daddy during birthing class. So that we knew what it would be like, they showed us a video of an actual birth. Clearly, this was a relatively smooth affair, and also much shorter than reality. Nonetheless, it was deliberately graphic, leaving no doubt as to what was going on.

In the video, the baby was delivered. The narrator continued, "and now Daddy can play a role. He is handed scissors and cuts the cord." My eyes rolled, "Oh please. That's it?" This hardly looked like an important role. It was tokenism at best.

To me what also appeared pretty simple was the "catching" job the obstetrician did. The baby came out; it was caught; everyone was relieved. Hardly rocket science.

It was time for me to step up and propose something real to do. Something necessary. Something involving potential risk. Something I could actually savor as an important life moment. I wanted to catch.

I suggested it to Child No. 1's mother-to-be. She knew me and played along. "Sure, let's put it to the obstetrician. If he says it's OK, you can do it." Her assumption (and mine too) was that he would object or, at the very least, require me to attend another round of birthing classes. That would likely put a stop to it. Catching may be life-savoring, but I wasn't going to go through that again.

So we asked him at our very next obstetrics appointment, and without any hesitation he said, "Of course!" Child No. 1's mother-to-be's jaw hit the floor, "Uh-oh." The "system" had not worked as she had hoped, but I was delighted. I began asking whether this was something regular. "Not regular, but it has happened."

Now as I psyched myself up for this, I anticipated the moment that I would hold my newborn daughter in my hands. I'd be the first person to hold her. She would know I was there. I would remember this moment forever.

Well, it didn't quite turn out that way. Practicalities were to impinge on my moment. It was about 3 a.m. We were in the last few stages of labor. What's more, there were two other women at the same stage at that time. We were actually alone until five minutes before Child No. 1 was born. I was saying, "Push!" I could see the head. And if need be, I could catch.

Eventually, the obstetrician rushed in. He told me that if I was going to do this, I had better get a gown and gloves on. Now to paint a picture of what happens next, think about a scene from a sitcom, say *Seinfeld*. Something serious is going on, but in the background one character (usually Kramer) is struggling alone with an issue in a comical manner. The tension makes the whole scene.

I went to put on the surgical gloves. I had never put those on before. As it turns out, it's not that easy. You have to struggle to get your fingers in, and then pull them down. All quite difficult at the best of times, let alone when you are rushing to get them on to catch your firstborn.

So there I was, Kramer-style, struggling and bouncing around the room, while in the background, the characters in the final birth event went on oblivious to my plight.

When the obstetrician yelled out to come over right now, I actually had to dive into the right place to have my hands ready for Child No. 1. It turned out to be a flying but successful catch—something that would really disturb you if you knew my catching skills for things like balls. She plopped onto my hands with gloves dangling over my fingers. The impact caused various stuff to splash back on me. The split second after I got her, she was quickly whisked away. My hands were left there with no baby, and I wondered what had become of my savoring moment. But I had done it. Something of no actual use, but nothing trivial either.

I went on to catch Child No. 2 with a noncomedic flair that could only come from having hours to practice putting on gloves. And I got my savoring moment. Child No. 3 came out far too quickly for me to even attempt it.

When I recount this to other expecting parents and inquire whether Daddy is going to catch, there is great resistance. One or the other of them wants Daddy to remain squarely at the other end of the event. But there is something really useful that you get from being more involved. Mommy never sees what is going on. You are a great source of information for her, and when you commit to being at the business end of the delivery bed, you can relay comforting thoughts back. And what is more, one of the parents gets to see their children emerge. Catching is one thing, but seeing that is quite another. When it comes down to it, that alone is a solid reason for Daddy to be present at the birth. It is the only way that particular memory can be created. I now have three.

PART II

THE BASICS

3 Sleeping

If you had asked me when I had a newborn what I wanted most for my child, I would have ranked health first, closely followed by sleep—for her, but mostly for ourselves. Sleep was our obsession during the first few months of our children's lives. Sure we enjoyed the babies, doted over them, and became excited at milestones. But those things just happen. Sleep was the activity that we as parents felt we should have some control over. So we engaged in enormous efforts to control it.

Success in such control can be mixed. I can see why some parents decide not to worry about it and just hope their child grows out of not sleeping. They opt for simple "solutions" like bringing the baby into bed. In many respects, this is just shifting the issue into the future. A few years later, someone will have to remove an older and more inconvenient child from their room.

Other parents try everything they can to get their child to sleep through the night independently. Sometimes, nothing works. The worst case I heard of was of a child who did not sleep more than a few hours each night. His mother needed counseling, and he didn't get a baby brother until many years later. Eventually, the child grew into a teenager, and the parents decided he could just stay up. That was simply the way he was.

In my mind, sleep is a negotiation. We want sleep, and the baby wants attention. There is an inherent conflict here. The screams of a baby are like an offer: "I'll stop screaming if you give me attention." And it is not a vague offer. Give the baby attention, and the crying stops. After only a few tries, a little baby can train its parents nicely.

In our sleep-obsessed state, our goal was to work out how to negotiate the price down. Counteroffers, such as, "If you would please just leave me alone until 6 a.m., I'll give you a car when you are sixteen," seemed to fall on deaf ears. Simple diplomacy, a meeting of the minds, a common understanding—none of these will work. Babies, it seems, cannot be reasoned with easily. It was hard to know what to do.

When I wrote about these matters on my blog, it provoked some strong reactions. It was put to me that my premise was all wrong. Why should parents want sleep? Why don't they do some nighttime parenting? Why are you so selfish? If you had a friend who needed your help, would you ignore them? Actually, if they needed my help several times a night for weeks, I think I would ignore them.

I felt it was perfectly reasonable to want sleep. Sleep deprivation harms your ability to parent well and also to work. I found it tough to spend any quality time with my child during the day as a zombie. Let's face it, zombies aren't known for their social and cognitive skills.

What's more, there is evidence that sleep deprivation can actually harm your health. New research has found what we all knew intuitively: a child's sleep habits and parental health are related. This includes not just mental health but physical health too. Australian researchers looked at ten thousand families and demonstrated that those with children who had sleep problems also had less healthy mothers and fathers.[1] The researchers used parents' past health histories to give them a benchmark for the impact of the child. This proved useful. Apparently, a mother who had never suffered depression was less prepared for the mental issues associated with a child's sleep issues. Fathers appeared to get away with just physical issues.

There is an important lesson here. Parents like us tend to focus on a child's sleep as the ultimate goal. It isn't. The goal was *our* sleep (free of interruption). Ultimately, what we wanted was for our child to leave us alone at night (except if they were in real distress, say related to sickness). Whether they happen to be asleep or not is a secondary issue. And when we came to negotiate with our baby, I found it useful to keep that in mind.[2]

The first step when you come to a negotiating table is to know the mind of your counterpart. An economist would advise you to construct a mental model of what their wants and needs are, and then to consider what information they have at their disposal. This will assist you in working out what you can push for.

To begin with, let's consider how people sleep. Basically, there's no such thing as sleeping through the night. Adults tend to wake up every 90 minutes. You don't notice because you fall back to sleep, and you can do this another five or six times. But babies have a different cycle, waking every sixty to seventy-five minutes.

According to Christopher Green, the phrase "sleeping like a baby" is misleading. When researchers examined video recordings of children as they "slept" at home:

> Parents of the children studied believed that their little ones were sleeping soundly right through the night, but the recordings showed otherwise. It appeared that even apparently good sleepers may wake a number of times to sit up, look around, play with their toys, kick off their covers, then perhaps have a quiet grizzle [whimper] before slipping back to sleep.[3]

This means that in order for you to get even a few uninterrupted hours, your child will have to go through one or more of these waking moments alone.

One obvious implication of this is that distance matters. If you have a baby in your bed, when they wake, they may disturb you. If you have a baby in a bassinet in your room, there is a similar risk. With a baby in a separate room, the baby has to put in more effort to make a disturbance. So, if you want to raise your chances of uninterrupted sleep, it will likely involve moving the baby away.

What this means is that, every hour or so, there is an opportunity for a child to "open up negotiations" with a starting offer. The goal is to make that not worth their while.

For a newborn baby, this is likely impossible. For starters, they have more they can legitimately complain about. They are learning to live outside the womb. That makes digestion a process to get used to. For many children, that can be painful. They express that pain by crying loudly and looking at you with eyes saying, "Hey you, don't just stand there, do something!" Absent pain medication, you end up doing things to distract them from their pain.

It turns out, those are things they tend to like even when there is no pain. At some point, a child learns this and starts using the same method to get a reaction from you. The trickery here is something you cannot hope to overcome. You can't distinguish between a cry for something they want and a cry for something they need. A baby playing their cards right can use this to their advantage. They can train you to give them attention at their whim.

It takes some weeks, but many parents soon start to suspect that something is up. By that time a shrewd baby has improved their acting skills. They can play with emotions, especially guilt, and will have you under their spell.[4] Now all this seems rather sinister, but there is a sense in which it helps to see babies in that way. They're human, you know, so they can be as manipulative and self-interested as the rest of us. Don't think you're negotiating with some sap.

The good news is that their showmanship comes at a price. It is not easy to cry, especially loudly. To do so effectively, you need to believe in your cause. Without that, a baby's acting skills can really wane. Our eldest child lost her ability to do this sometime through her second year. Her attempts at crying were feeble, indeed laughable. And laugh we did! Suffice it to say, we did not see it very often. In contrast, Child No. 2 was able to really feel for his cause. He was far more credible, but, given the emotional cost, it was also something he couldn't do often. Nonetheless, he got away with more. Child No. 3 got the acting down beautifully. She could bring Meryl Streep to tears. But she used it too often, and we were on to it. We could literally tell her to stop crying. She would then cough and stop. That was quite the party trick, especially in front of other parents.

The cost of crying (in terms of the baby's exertion) means that it will only continue as long as a baby can reasonably expect it to work. This is the philosophy behind the "controlled crying" technique for parents with sleep issues. Popularized by Richard Ferber,[5] controlled crying is all about breaking a baby's association between their crying and your reaction. The idea is to make sure that when they are in bed, they learn to do things that are independent of you. What this ultimately means is that, at some point, you just have to let them cry.

The theory is simple. It has to be if you are going to "explain" it to a baby. If you make a big deal about bedtime and associate it with things that require your attention, then that is what will happen. Bedtime is a first foray into independence and, of course, it is a rare baby who doesn't react to that.

After all, from their perspective they are the center of the universe—and everything else about their lives at the time reinforces that belief.

Pediatrician Sydney Spiesel[6] puts it this way:

> My advice to parents in my practice is based on my sense that children wake in the middle of the night seeking the reward of the warmth and affection they have come to expect. In twenty-five years practicing as a pediatrician, I've found that mothers in particular are often as reluctant as children to give up the nighttime cuddle. It is, after all, a time of pure and intense pleasure with a child, free of worries about hurting someone else's feelings or the need to put breakfast on the table or to answer the phone. The problem, of course, is that eventually the early-hours pleasure makes mothers miserable in the morning. When you get to that point—and if your baby is at least four months old—it may be time to decrease the child's reward for waking so as to make it not worth the trouble.

From your baby's perspective, attention at nighttime is a bonus. To stop them wanting to claim it, you have to take it off the table.

Implementing this is hard, especially for first-time parents. You're not necessarily equipped to manage it on your own and might need to get some support.

That is what happened to us. Child No. 1 spent the first six weeks of her life not sleeping. We were getting four-hour breaks at best. I was hallucinating. (I saw a horse running on the freeway and still remember it vividly!) We took her over to a friend's place. They had more children. We put her down, and they stopped us from going into the room. Thirty minutes later she was asleep.

That night we implemented a hard line. The baby monitor was screaming. Child No. 1's mother said that she couldn't stand listening to it anymore. So I went to the monitor and turned it off. "Problem solved." Ten minutes later, we determined with our ears to the door that the baby was asleep. Four hours later we didn't get her; she screamed and then went back to sleep. Eight hours after that we woke up, panicked, and ran to her room. She was lying there happily smiling at us. She had been awake but we were not. A deal had been struck.

We never had another problem night from her again. And when I say never, I mean *never*. She would go down at 6:30 p.m. and stay there until 6:30 a.m. Twelve hours per night without fail. Now it wasn't just the hard line that allowed this but also the fact that we made sure she wasn't hungry. Every day, between 4 p.m. and 6 p.m., we engaged in what we called a "feeding frenzy." She would drink almost continuously for that period of time. Then we had a bath, a story, and bed. It wouldn't work for every child, but with that mix and that child we definitely got results.

There was one wrinkle. The idea was to get her to put herself back to sleep without us. Initially, we used a pacifier for this purpose. The problem was that it would fall out. Her room was dark. I can only imagine her experience of crying out, suddenly feeling some large hands groping around her face for a hole and then having a pacifier shoved in her mouth. If it doesn't sound pleasant to you, you won't be surprised that it only took her a couple of weeks to find her built-in pacifier: her thumb.

That was something we would have to deal with a few years later to save her future teeth. It was a small price to pay.

There can be some delicateness to all this. A crying baby can quickly become a tired baby. And when they become overtired, even the small amount of reason you are trying to inject can go out the window. In this situation, they may be unable to calm down without assistance. From their perspective, they have won.

This leads to something that is counter to your instincts. Rather than putting your baby down when they appear tired, put them to bed when they are awake—perhaps half an hour before you expect them to be tired. At that time your negotiations will have a better chance of succeeding. Sure, the first few times you leave a happy and awake baby in their crib, they will be confused and scream to be returned to their previous position. But that process will also not leave them overtired as they learn to understand your new negotiating position.

This also allows you to do things a bit more gradually than the Ferber line. Not a big bang, half-hour session; instead, maybe ten minutes first, followed by some attention. But, above all, you need to set things up such that the baby is committed to the crib. They are not picked up, the light does not come on, and there is certainly no food. Perhaps when you first put them down to sleep, you can turn on some music so that the association is complete. The point is that in the end, if you don't want interruptions, their reward for waking up has to be entirely removed.

So how did all this knowledge translate to Child No. 2? After all, we were experienced with this now and had seen results. For him, it was a hard line pretty much from the start. And the result was eight-plus hours of sleep each night at four weeks. I began to think that perhaps I should write a book on parenting!

Alas, it didn't last. This was not a sleep issue but an eating one. Child No. 1 had been a great eater (straight from four months, the recommended time at the turn of the millennium to introduce solids). When we put Child No. 2 on solids, he enjoyed it so much that we got overenthusiastic. Then he got stomach cramps, had to be taken off food, and didn't sleep through properly again until ten months.

Sleep performance does, to a large extent, depend upon the child. Child No. 1 was well suited to it. She ate like a pig, and that meant she could get enough fuel into her before bed to last through the night. She also is a heavy sleeper. To this day (she is now nine) we can move her around in her sleep without her noticing.

On the other hand, Child No. 2 would throw up his evening meal all the time and was a light sleeper. He also didn't need as much sleep. To this day, he bounds out of bed at 5 a.m., ready to go. He is the ultimate morning person—even before it's officially morning! Compared with Child No. 1, who thinks that morning is an affront to her rights and grumps for a good hour, our son is disturbingly happy and cheery at sunrise.

So what of Child No. 3? Again, we used a hard-line approach from the start (partly because we didn't realize the old baby monitor wasn't working too well, so we got our "spine" for free; we simply didn't know she was crying—oops!).

In terms of results, we got nothing we would count as "sleeping through" until eight months. This was because our daughter reached a compromise solution. She wanted five minutes of our time sometime between midnight and 2 a.m. for a feed, and that was it. We hardly felt it, and when it comes down to it we effectively got 90 percent of the Ferber-type independence anyway.

Nowadays when she wakes up at the crack of dawn she is greeted first by Child No. 2, who, let's face it, is the right person for the job. That buys us extra sleep time.

A hard-line negotiating approach has lots of merits, but it is implementation that you have to concentrate on. Absent that, a defective baby monitor will work wonders.

Sometimes the problems persist beyond the toddler years. At this time, more traditional and explicit negotiating techniques are at the parents' disposal. Once again, the issue is that the child wants attention. The critical thing here is that the bonus or reward has to be truly rewarding, rather than something that is freely available.

A potential solution owes much to the economics of property rights. Research suggests that by giving a child a free pass, sleep issues can be substantially reduced.[7] A *free pass* is a card the child can exchange after bedtime for, say, leaving their room to get a drink (a common delaying tactic) or a parental hug. Basically, by limiting the number of passes a child has, you limit the quantity of disruptions they can get away with, without having to resort to an outright ban. It turns out that sticking with a free pass technique yields a substantial improvement in bedtime tantrums and other nighttime interruptions. And the gains are sustained well beyond the free pass era.

There are some good basic economics behind this. But you would have to keep strictly to the pass system. Relent early on and it would surely fall apart. Hopefully, it works just as well for parents without a set of researchers to report back to.

Some sleep issues with children come from having to fit in with society. A good example of this is society's adherence to a standardized time.

Every year, we stop daylight saving time and start spending it again. We do so until the daylight deficit grows too much and, in one sharp shock, go back into surplus six months later.

Both the beginning and the end of daylight saving are generally good news for parents, for about a week; but this is because the month preceding them is usually bad. The problem we face is that young children are particularly disrespectful of time standards. They are already set in their ways, and many rise with the sun and then refuse to sleep until it has gone down. Now effective "within-room" light management can give you a measure of control, but it is rarely perfect.

What this means is that, by the end of summer, your child is going to bed later than you want, and it is also hard to get them up for school in the morning. So the end of daylight saving time is a blessing. For about a week, they will drop off to sleep nicely and also be easy to get up in the morning; in our household that is something we value, but I could see why others might not.

Of course, this can all go too far. By spring, we face the opposite problem. Then the sun is rising very early—and with it, the children. This means that by the end of the day, they can be quite ratty. The start of daylight saving is a sensible adjustment to what the earth in its orbit of the sun is dictating.

When it comes to these sorts of problems with children sleeping, society is to blame. If your child is getting up at what society claims is 4:30 a.m., that is only an issue for you because you have a meeting at 8:30 a.m. If your meeting were at 6:30 a.m. instead, there would be no difference between the child waking up at 4:30 or two hours later. The meeting time should really be adjusted to fit in with the sleep patterns, which after all are biological and no one's fault.

True freedom would allow us to keep our own time and have others adjust accordingly. Would it be so bad if we all followed a schedule based on sunrise and sunset rather than on artificial time? Time shifting TV schedules by using DVRs and VCRs has already allowed us to achieve this in small measure.

Now before you start thinking I'm against daylight saving, let me say that what I'm really arguing for is *continual* daylight saving and spending. Not radical hourly shocks twice a year, but continuous readjustment. We could somehow sync all our clocks via the Internet, and everyone would just find out the time in the usual way. The timekeeper (I think, at the moment, that is the U.S. vice president) would dictate what time it was, with minor adjustments taking place every night. No one would know the difference, and we wouldn't have to remember to adjust our clocks. The full energy-saving and lifestyle benefits of daylight saving would be realized, and we would be aligned with nature so that parents wouldn't have to hold out for the clocks to change. A truly responsive society would give us that much.

4 Eating

Gluttony is an unusual sin—if it should even be called that—because the only person you are harming is probably yourself. Now when there is a food shortage, gluttony harms others because you are taking more than you need. But in most modern societies, this isn't really an issue.

These days, there are often newspaper reports trying to justify a modern-day "harm-to-others" impact from gluttony. It usually comes through the extra burden the nongluttons face in their health care costs. A potentially fair argument, especially where there is a public health system, but really, the main health costs are borne by the individuals themselves. No one looks at Augustus Gloop in *Charlie and the Chocolate Factory* and worries about his impact on society. Indeed, it is hard to be concerned even about his impact on himself. But if one looks to blame someone, his parents loom large.

One of our parental tasks is to teach our children how to eat well and sensibly. This is easier said than done, because not only do we not necessarily eat sensibly ourselves, sometimes we don't even know how to do it. What is more, the information out there as to what is healthy is constantly changing. One year eggs are bad; the next year they're good again. When I was growing up, my parents forced me to drink orange juice every morning. For my kids, juice is forbidden, and when they taste it they believe it to be the nectar of the gods.

There are two great regulators of good eating: habit and guilt. By eating certain foods, I get used to them. If I eat less, my stomach shrinks. If I eat less meat, I find it hard to stomach more. If I eat less sugar, my stomach growls less. So having good habits can be self-sustaining.

But there is only so far that can go. As with all such things, there is the possibility of "chipping." Temptation arrives, and I have a little bit. That can be fine except that what is little can grow into more. It may take some time, but a healthy eater can become an unhealthy one. To stop you chipping away at a habitual healthy diet, a healthy dose of guilt is needed.

Guilt is the moderator of gluttony. That is why it has its sin status. If you were to take me as an example, guilt might not seem much of a moderator. It's there; it's just not perfect. Every time that something delicious yet unhealthy tempts me, a pang of guilt accompanies it. It takes the edge off the deliciousness and more often than not causes me to forbear. And the guilt is not for guilt's sake. It is a reflection of training, of knowing that I need moderation for good health, and more recently, good health for the sake of my children. You might think that last manifestation of uberguilt would be sufficient to have me quite thin indeed (it has certainly done wonders for my children's mother), but that is not to be. Guilt moderates; it does not eliminate.

Those things aside, guilt plays a large role when it comes to children and eating. It will come about in several manifestations in this chapter—from maternal guilt and breast-feeding, to how to encourage healthy eating by guilt-free children, to, finally, a tension between guilt and some basic reward systems that are part of the potential toolkit. From an economic perspective, guilt is created as an "internal price" that we pay for certain eating choices. But, as we will learn, without a market to moderate that price, it is hard to get it right.

The issue of kids and eating hits home immediately after birth. Although it has gone through cycles, these days many health organizations extol the virtues of breast-feeding. There are economic studies that talk about the billions that would be saved on health care if, say, 20 percent more babies were breast-fed.[1] But again, as with most dietary matters, there is confusion.

It turns out that, like many situations where science is translated for public consumption, the virtues of breast-feeding might be overstated. For instance, during nursing time in our household, it was common for us to cheer on the wonderful antibodies that were coming down through the breast milk. But apparently, these antibodies get as far as the baby's stomach and there they stay. Although they do good work there—preventing diarrhea (the grossness-saving value of which cannot be underestimated)—they don't seem to prevent other stuff.[2] And what is more, breast milk may generate other benefits, but, as no one has been willing to take random babies and deny them breast milk, we don't really know.

In many respects, I am glad that we didn't know all of that while our children were feeding, especially at the beginning. Breast-feeding appears to be hard. Really hard. The image from *The Blue Lagoon* where Brooke Shields's baby just worked it all out is pure fantasy. A baby has instincts but an incomplete awareness of the world. The mother has to train her child to breast-feed properly and in a nonpainful way. It can be physically, mentally, and emotionally draining.

One of the worst nights we ever had was the night we brought our firstborn home from the hospital. While the nurses were around, breast-feeding was working just fine, so we thought it would be all right at home, too. But at 3 a.m., Child No. 1 was not being a cooperative eater, and the consequences of a day's worth of bad habits had caught up on some poor breasts. Feeding was too painful, but our baby, quite understandably, was screaming. We were at a loss. In the end, we decided to make use of a breast pump—something we could control. But, while the milk was being bottled, I held the baby a little too close to my nose and, well, boy did that hurt. It was a fleeting dose of empathy.

Now I don't want to give the impression that I am against breast-feeding or to discourage it. For starters, the idea that a mother might produce a milk product that is better for her baby than formula makes a lot of sense. In addition, once you get it right, it really is convenient. Purchasing, mixing, and then packing formula for times away from home is another cost and chore you could do without. It is so much easier to have a built-in, portable system.

Of course, it is only built-in for one parent. Breast-feeding is also supposed to save on sterilization, but that wasn't the case with us. For sanity as well as career reasons, we needed an independent supply of milk. So an area of the kitchen was cordoned off to become the "clean zone." You were not allowed to breathe there. It was there that the equipment and bottles were kept sterile. Then our freezer was filled with dozens of little bags of precious liquid. And being the dispenser of this liquid, woe betide me if I should lose a drop.

During our baby days, we must have had a three weeks' supply in there. It was a good thing too, because when Child No. 3 was ten months old, she was hospitalized and could not breast-feed. The stocks were run down, but a few months of extra feeding were possible.

Because breast-feeding is such a difficult activity, especially at the beginning, guilt is an important driver. Basically, from birth on, breast-feeding has an *option value*. If it can be done, then you have the option to keep going with it. If you choose not to breast-feed in the early days, there is no going back. Guilt focuses you on the future, which is where the real value of an extra feeding comes from. And in a sleep-deprived state, guilt can help substitute for a lack of attention to the future.[3]

The rest of the societal pressure really serves no useful function. Reports about saving health costs are fine but may not be accurate or relevant. In any case, if the primary benefits of breast-feeding are gastronomical, then parents have ample incentive to capture them. Indeed, breast-feeding should not be seen as the only way to do that.

Some societal pressure, in many respects, is applied too late. By the time parents are back in the world, with their feeding choices on display, breast-feeding has either become easy or it didn't work out. The social pressure serves no useful function. Perhaps we should just be grateful that in modern society we have other options.

Breast milk and formula are one issue; food is quite another. And very soon after you introduce solids, a simple issue emerges: how do you make sure what they eat is healthy?

The key flash point in the battle over food is, of course, vegetables. Kids eating their vegetables evoke all that is good in nutrition. We feel that if we could manage that, we'd have succeeded. But what we actually want is a balanced diet.

When a child first starts eating, you have a bit more control. Basically, the first bit of solids you give them is some pasty rice cereal that has no taste. At that stage, the child has no discrimination. They don't know what they're missing. What's more, you can progressively introduce foods and tastes. Usually fruit first, but then *vegetables*.

Now some children plough through this introduction quite nicely. For us, Child No. 1 would eat anything she was given from about the age of four months. Child No. 2 was the same. His problem was that his stomach couldn't handle it. So at five months, we took him off solids for a month and slowly reintroduced them later. By the time Child No. 3 showed up a few years later, the official starting date for solids had shifted to six months. And a good thing too.

From the outset, Child No. 3 was more discriminating. She liked fruit and dairy products but appeared to hate vegetables. I would sit there feeding her fruit and then switch to carrots. Her face contorted in shock, and she would refuse anything more. I'd have to put some fruit on her tongue to get her eating again. Then, just as she was comfortable, I would slip another dose of the healthy stuff in.

Now this would have worked quite well in terms of a balanced diet if she hadn't cottoned on to the strategy; soon she began to refuse any food at all from me. My reputation had been shot. I'd have to behave myself in the future.

Anyway, our babies ate well. It was just a matter of balancing the diet somehow, and we would be fine. But for other parents, if the baby really doesn't eat much, then just getting food in can be a struggle. And it is here that the slippage from unliked to liked food comes in. However, once a child can actually look at some food and forecast its taste, the old game is over, and a brand new one begins.

The first thing you notice about kids and eating is the absence of guilt. All of the guilt mechanisms adults incorporate are absent. What is more, putting them there is a lost cause. The old adage of "Eat it. Don't you know kids are starving in [insert country here]?" is more memorable for its lack of effectiveness than the guilt pangs it generates. The idea was that you shouldn't waste your food, because others were doing without. That prompted the sensible response: "Well, let's send these peas there then! I'm not stopping you."

As they get older, school indoctrination starts to work for you. Recently, Child No. 1 has responded to "health concerns" and will now eat vegetables based on the argument that she needs a balanced diet. This is great, but let's face it, not many kids are going to buy that one. After all, it's a tough sell to adults!

That said, nothing has improved my diet more than the demonstration effect. To get the children to eat well, we have to eat well too. Whether we like it or not, our plates need to be cleaned. I must admit that I still hold out on the drink front and have a Coke with my dinner. That serves as another useful opportunity for moral persuasion: "You can have water. You don't want to end up like Daddy, do you?"

While some research suggests that, left to their own devices, kids might actually balance out their diet themselves,[4] healthy eating is generally reached through negotiation. In this process, it is important to get right who is selling what. It is easy to get caught up with the idea that you are selling health to your children, but that path leads to a marketing campaign on peas and carrots. It just won't work.

Instead, you need to consider yourself as the seller of unhealthy foods—chocolate and ice cream. And you have to be shrewd at it. You need to try and get your customers (the children) to give you the best possible price for your wares.

By "price" I don't mean money but, of course, healthy eating. They supply that product. So just as a farmer might go to market and exchange some cattle for a plow, you approach your children with unhealthy food in exchange for healthy eating. Of course, to buy some healthy eating you could also rely on video games, television, and other restricted pursuits. But these do not have the immediacy and association that food has.

Perhaps the most direct route is to bundle the unhealthy and healthy food together, in much the same way that a movie theater offers you a big drink with your popcorn. You can take the vegetables and cover them in something more pleasing to your child's taste buds. At the age of two, Child No. 3 was very receptive to this deal. Indeed, we could feed her cardboard so long as there was tomato sauce available. But mixing something healthy with something not so healthy seems to defeat the purpose. It also makes it hard to adjust the rate of exchange. (That is, the amount of stuff you have to eat relative to the amount of tasty stuff you get.) It will always be two parts vegetable, one part sauce.[5] What you really want is a deal with more monetary control, so that you can slowly improve the ratio of healthy to unhealthy eating—literally, preventing inflation. (Don't you just love economic puns!)

Actually, for a time, our surefire way of getting Child No. 3 to eat well was to put vegetables on our own plate and not give them to her. She would complain and then happily eat from our plates as if she had won some sort of prize. The "grass is greener" effect was useful, but it turned out to be short-lived.

At the opposite end of the bundling strategy is an extreme form of deprivation; I guess one would call it starvation. We've discovered that when, on busy days, we forget to feed the kids a usual meal (like lunch), boy do they eat their dinner well! It turns out that hunger is a great motivator. Alas, for obvious reasons, it can't really be deployed intentionally. Nonetheless, it did give us comfort that, if we held out for a meal or two, they would eventually eat some healthy food.

As a peddler of unhealthy food, there are some good economic strategies you can use to get the price up. The first is to try, where possible, to supply low-quality merchandise rather than the good stuff. If your children love to eat, their desire for quantity can be a weakness. So in return for vegetable eating, you can offer them second and third courses with, say, meat and then fruit. That promise may well be enough to get them through the vegetable part.

This strategy has worked very well for Child No. 1, in particular, who never stops eating. For her, not getting through the vegetables carries a second penalty of not getting enough to eat overall. This adds up to bargaining strength on our part, and we use it mercilessly. Indeed, we've found we actually have to limit her food intake to three courses just to ensure we get through meals in a timely fashion.

But for most normal children it is a harder sell. For them, there are two important strategies: keeping the good stuff scarce and utilizing good marketing. I'll come to marketing in a moment, but, in general, that is secondary to the issue of just how much unhealthy stuff is going around.

As any good monopolist knows, if you want to jack up the price, keep supply short. Certainly, having limited supplies of treats in the house is a start. But it can go too far. If there are none around, the child might not believe any will be forthcoming. Our children are savvy enough to negotiate upfront. If the goods ain't around at dinner time, any promises otherwise may not be credible. So there had better be some supply on hand.

Once again, as any monopolist knows, the main threats to supply come from others. Parties, school, grandparents, and others all offer treats at the "can't refuse price" of zero. They do this because they don't face the same internal "costs" (i.e., guilt) that help you keep goods off the street. What's more, every treat supplied for free to your child is a lost opportunity to do a deal later on.

Child No. 1, who is extremely receptive to the healthy for unhealthy food deal, will take any opportunity to fill up when the going is good. She loves both types of food too much, so her price is correspondingly, and somewhat embarrassingly (from an economist dad's perspective), low. We often arrive at parties to find her sitting alone at the table savoring popcorn, juice, and chips while all the other kids have run off to do more interesting things. For each of her own birthdays, we have a sad-looking photo of her sitting alone at a big, empty party table. What is sadder I guess is that, in her deprived state, she recalls these as her happier moments.

So, as parents, we rightly get upset when treats are supplied by others. Our control is undermined. But what I don't understand is that in our household there seems to be an exception to all this when it comes to home-cooked treats. On weekends, there is a steady stream of muffins, brownies, and cookies coming from the kitchen. This is not my handiwork. Instead, their mother gathers them up for cooking sessions. Not surprisingly, they are willing participants in "quality time" with Mommy. Not only are there treats at the end, but there is a heap of spoon and bowl licking in between.

Now you have to realize that, when it comes to food enforcement, Mommy is normally the strict one. She is constantly upping the price, with more and more exotic vegetables at dinnertime and less and less of the more pleasant-tasting healthy food. We all suffer under that regime. But when it comes to home cooking, it all goes out the window. I questioned her about this and heard claims from "I know what's going into it" to "They enjoy spending time with me doing activities." Yeah, but they aren't giving love, they're selling it. And when it comes down to it, at some level, home production is just as bad as outside purchases in undermining the whole incentive system. But for my part, I do enjoy those warm, fresh-from-the-oven chocolate chip cookies.

The other tool in a seller's arsenal is marketing. This is where you do things that push up the value of what you're selling. When it comes to unhealthy food, this might seem strange. Marketing would require you to actually promote chocolate and ice cream as wonderful things rather than deride them.

If this seems somewhat counter to the whole exercise, let me explain. What you're trying to do is get your children to eat more vegetables and less ice cream. If they don't think that ice cream is tasty, then in exchange for eating, say, three pieces of carrot, you will have to give them one ice cream cone. In contrast, if your child thinks ice cream is, like, the best thing ever, you can get them to eat carrots for a whole week before doling out the special treat.

Now I don't expect parents to go around and torture their children by dangling very yummy-looking treats in front of them—although that is consistent with the economics of the situation. Instead, you might like to think differently about the type of promotion the food industry uses to sell food to kids.

These days it is popular for politicians to decry the advertising of food to children. They see it as leading to childhood obesity and the like. Of course, if a child is able to arrange their own food supply, then such advertising isn't going to help matters. But in situations where parents have a tight control on supply, the advertising is great.

For starters, advertising allows someone else to promote the unhealthy goods, without you becoming a hypocrite and potentially undermining the whole philosophy behind the deal you are trying to strike. But there's more. Advertising doesn't put any more sugar in the treats, but it does put more sugar in children's heads. The better they *think* the treat is going to be, the more good stuff I can get into them in return.

Give me pure, puffy advertising and a *Shrek* label any day. If having a green character on a chocolate bar means a child will be as happy with a 1 ounce treat as a 2 ounce one, then so much the better. Shrek is an ally in my quest to market unhealthy goods to my children. Put simply, you want treats to have a good taste and leave a good memory without much being eaten.

I also wince at moves that would limit McDonald's ability to put toys in with Happy Meals. That is hitting on the wrong problem. Happy Meals are not about the food—they're about the toys. The good thing about the food is that it is in small quantities (three nuggets rather than six, and no large size). In my day, when we went to McDonald's, we would eat adult meals. Anything that stops that is surely a good thing. McDonald's is likely making all their money on selling the toys in these meals.

For the same reason, such marketing doesn't work for healthy stuff. Sure, by dancing along with *The Wiggles* you can make it a bit more exciting, but in the end that pushes up the food price for you and gives you an excuse to buy less.

And if we are worried about children eating McDonald's, then the biggest threat—ironically—are the salads and sandwiches McDonald's now offers. These make it easier to sell Happy Meals. Why?

Previously, a constraint on going to McDonald's was that increasingly health-conscious adults would resist because they'd have nothing to eat. That is no longer the case, so more children will get McDonald's. I don't want to suggest banning healthy food at McDonald's—only that playing around with these things is complicated.

So, let's not forget the critical role junk food plays in child discipline and incentives. Every time an ad is shown, children value junk food more and therefore react more when they receive it as a reward. Happy Meals do have carrots after all.

5 Toileting

Children, it turns out, can work out how to do lots of things on their own. Crawling and walking are obvious candidates. Eating is also right up there. But some kids teach themselves to do much more complex things, like reading. This, of course, makes one wonder what all the parental effort is for. Usually, the best that can be said is that it speeds things up a little.

Nothing, however, taxes a parent's energy like toilet training. If a child reads a year later, it usually doesn't affect much. But taking a year longer to learn how to go to the toilet is very costly. Even aside from the obvious costs of diapers and various cleaning routines, there comes a time when a parent feels enough is enough (usually somewhere around the six thousandth diaper change). After attending to your child's personal waste for years, you feel it is time for some independence.

It is a rare case, indeed, that a child works this out for themselves. The best example I heard of was a mother who noticed that her six-month-old (!) seemed to be doing a "number two" at the same time every day (because of the smelly "insult," as they term it in the diaper business). So, to save herself some trouble, she'd hold the child over the toilet. This went on for months while the child still wore diapers. The diapers were never soiled, but the mother thought it was just luck.

Then one weekend they went away and left the routine at home. The child didn't go all weekend (much to her parents' alarm), which was how they worked out that, at least for the worst insults, she had been trained.

For normal children (that is, all the rest), there is no such luck. The pressures to act build up quickly. At two or so years, your child is starting to look like a real person. And, let's face it, in a short while that diaper bottom will start to look obvious. Soon enough, they'll need to attend kindergarten, before which they need to be certified as independent, toilet-trained individuals. Later on there are school, sleepovers, and marriage. If the cord isn't cut, none of those things will be available to them. But here you have a child with no interest whatsoever in abandoning the cushy, full-service attention they have enjoyed their entire life. They just don't understand the urgency here. The clock is ticking.

At this point someone pipes up, "I think we should start potty training junior this weekend." Then the other one says, "Let me look at my schedule. Hmm, I have to travel for work, but it sounds good to me!"

So begins a discussion of the plan, the timeline, and the incentives. Even if you somehow delude yourself that you don't need incentives, your child generally has other ideas. It is all much easier said than done.

One issue I should raise right at the start is that this is all partly the fault of the comfortable disposable diaper. In the olden days—say, three decades ago—cloth diapers were the repository of choice. These had the feature that when they were wet, everyone knew it. Parents knew it, but the child also felt the discomfort.

As the child grew older, the discomfort grew with them. The causal link between what they were doing, in a bodily function sense, and the discomfort was felt early and often. Thus, not only did parents want their child out of these things quickly, the child was on board too.

The disposable diaper has changed that relationship. It is a remarkable piece of technology. Author Malcolm Gladwell believes that it is an achievement that ranks alongside the microchip:

> We tend to credit those who create an idea, not those who perfect it, forgetting that it is often only in the perfection of an idea that true progress occurs. Putting sixty-four transistors on a chip allowed people to dream of the future. Putting four million transistors on a chip actually gave them the future. The diaper is no different. The paper diaper changed parenting. But a diaper that could hold four insults without leakage, keep a baby's skin dry, clear an insult [which is actually what you think it is] in twenty seconds flat, and would nearly always

> be in stock, even if you arrived at the supermarket at eight o'clock in the evening—and that would keep getting better at all those things, year in and year out—was another thing altogether. This was more than a good idea. This was something like perfection.[1]

It is like perfection because while the technology does its job, it also affects the parent and the child. The parent, not surprisingly, wants to employ a disposable diaper right away. Sometimes they buy the propaganda that not having a cloth diaper might lead to training issues later on. We did this for the first few days of Child No. 1, but we don't talk about such foolishness anymore.

But for the child, it is comfort that can continue forever. When they are told it is time for the diaper to go, the expression on their face says it all. They appreciate the beauty and functionality of the design. Perhaps they also suspect they will be wearing one again in seventy or so years' time. Why deny them in the interim?

The unintended consequence of the disposable diaper is that it changed the "toilet or not" cost equation for the child. Incentive issues arise from a misalignment of interests. The disposable diaper was something both parent and child wanted, but when it comes to taking it away, their relative benefits are quite different.

Now this issue has occurred to many a parent at the toilet-training stage of the modern child. I, for one, wondered whether an electrically fitted diaper could be constructed that would administer a short, sharp shock when wet. Others have suggested a powder that becomes itchy when wet. Somewhat less torturously, the latest training pants (that is, diapers a child can pull up and down by themselves) have a liner in them so that a child can feel the wetness immediately. That may help them associate the physical act with its result, but it's still far from incentive alignment.

No, if you want to take the diaper away, these days there are few options but to manage the whole exercise. And that requires thinking about the incentives.

In our three experiences with all this, we have tried various things and each time been presented with new challenges. The notion that no two children are alike—despite genetic similarity—comes to the fore here.

Toilet training is an exercise in behavior modification: you try to convince an otherwise happy and contented child that they have to take responsibility for their own actions—namely toileting. It is a classic situation where the interests of one party (the parents) differ from those of the other (the child). If you want to align those interests, someone is going to have to pay up. The only question is, how much? What reward do you need to offer to get the behavior you want?

Enter Child No. 1. Despite my economics background, we decided that, initially, we would bid low and see if we could get away with it. We thought we would appeal to some broad, vague sense that it would be good to grow up and wouldn't that be "exciting." Not surprisingly, those claims had about the same impact as calls for whiter, brighter towels or peace on Earth, or what have you.

So it wasn't long before the price started to rise. But how do you engage in shameless bribery with a two-year-old? There isn't a lot to work with there. While money can appeal by about the age of eight, for the younger ones you have to appeal to a base motive. All we could think of was food; in particular, "special" food.

It was fortunate that we had decided at some earlier point—several weeks earlier—to make a distinction between general food (food that we would always allow our daughter to have) and special food (food that we would virtually never allow her to have). Into the former category fell rice cakes, fruit, yogurt, chicken, and all vegetables. Into the latter category fell just about everything else. So now we had lots to work with. But here's a hint for the unprepared: engage in some pre-training deprival. It creates its own reward.

We decided to begin with jelly beans. The basic reward was to give out jelly beans for successful toileting behavior. You got one or two jelly beans depending upon what you did, with one for . . . and I'm sure you can guess the rest.

But the whole scheme went further. You see, the jelly bean may be the reward, but game theory teaches us that unless the "incentive contract" (that link between action and reward) is clearly communicated, it won't work. So we didn't simply have a bag of beans that we took out of the cupboard when required. Nor did we rely on a pretty chart to record success. Instead, we installed a whole publicly displayed apparatus. It stood atop a kitchen counter. When you wanted a jelly bean, you had to push a button. This started everything but a song and dance, following which a single jelly bean was dispensed.

Now this is all very well, but right at the beginning the child isn't going to engage in any behavior that demonstrates how the whole deal works. Demonstration is the key. To overcome this, we decided to apply the reward universally. That is, anyone—including us and our guests—would be entitled to a jelly bean as they emerged from the bathroom.

For weeks, I would emerge from the bathroom to find my daughter standing outside, asking me if I was allowed one or two jelly beans. If we forgot to take one, we would be reminded. Outsiders could monitor the whole household's performance as they came in: "Looking a bit empty there; better cut down on the coffee."

Did this work? It certainly put the whole issue on the table, and our daughter showed much interest in spending time on the potty. But, after a couple of weeks, we had little to show for it except a personal dislike of jelly beans, as their consumption came to us to be associated with unpleasant activities. We made a conscious effort to disguise our toileting activities to avoid having to eat any more!

At this point, we had to contemplate a ratcheting up of the reward—to chocolate frogs. This was a decision we did not take lightly, as we were well aware that at some point we would want to end our little incentive contract. But we knew that if anything was going to get the behavior we wanted, it would be this; we could work on our exit strategy later.

To a casual observer, it did the trick. While precious few jelly beans had been awarded to our daughter, she was now getting two or three chocolate frogs a day. Moreover, we started saving on diapers.

Alas, a more careful audit of our household performance would show dubious results. Our daughter realized that there was a very easy way she could acquire a frog. In her time-rich life, she would simply wait. Basically, she worked out that if you sit on the toilet long enough, something will happen. And so she did this, for hours and hours on end.

Now we let this go on for a while in the hope she would get a feeling for her own bodily functions. But it was starting to get worrying and to interfere with normal daily activities. So when she didn't appear to tire of these activities, we changed the reward. She was only allowed to sit on the toilet for short (!) half-hour bursts.

This all worked and, after a week, she began to anticipate her needs. In a flurry of activity we could make it to the toilet, and there was much rejoicing. Although that gave rise to a new issue. Our daughter worked out—as many kids do—that this was a way to instantly gain attention.

I recall one such incident at a department store. I was buying some clothes, and my daughter announced that she had to go to the bathroom. Her mother scooped her up immediately and asked the sales clerk where the toilet was. She was told that she would have to go outside into the mall. "Well, that is just great. You are going to end up with wee all over your floor." And then she fled, having pushed the hapless clerk out of the way in violent protest.

Upon their return, some fifteen minutes later, it was discovered that all this was a false alarm. It was then that we developed a greater sense of calm about all of this, including how to cope with the same "I need to go" announcements in the car on the freeway. What can you do? It turns out that she always held it in.

Nonetheless, during all this training, no sooner had we fixed one problem than another began; she got too much control! Our daughter realized that by holding back, she could convert one trip to the toilet into two or three, and thus triple her frog consumption. Tim Harford[2] likens this effect to the way pole-vaulter Sergei Bubka, who was paid a cash bonus each time he broke the world record, chose to do it a centimeter at a time. That's the risk you face when you set down clear, objective rules for rewards: you often get what you pay for.

There are two reactions to such gaming. If our daughter was an employee and we were trying to reward her for performance we wanted, we might promise a reward if she obtained a "favorable" evaluation. The problem here is that, to avoid gaming, the evaluation cannot be clearly defined. You actually want it to say something like: "You get a chocolate frog when you go to the toilet in an appropriate and sustainable manner." Suffice it to say, employees don't often buy this type of deal, let alone children. Discretion makes those being rewarded wary of your commitment to paying up.

So we opted for an alternative course. We decided to phase out the reward program. This was not done without some fear: what if removing the system eliminated all our good work? But we did it slowly, first by increasing her quota (the period of time over which she had to exclusively use the toilet before getting a frog), and then removing the reward entirely.

Suffice it to say, there was no reversion, and all in all we were happy with the outcome. Eventually, the motive we initially hoped for—getting out of diapers and into more exciting underpants—took over. But the management process was painful, and I can't prove whether this wouldn't have all happened of its own accord anyway, without rewards. Such is the nature of the first child.

Now you might have thought that all of this experience with Child No. 1 might have meant that things would be a little easier with Child No. 2. One thing we planned on doing was waiting a little longer before we started toilet training, and checking for more signs of readiness. Then we would go for a "big bang" behavioral change.

Alas, training our son proved to be a very different ball game from training our first daughter—and not simply due to gender differences, which some believe are significant in these things. You see, our daughter possessed several qualities that helped us when applying incentives. First, she was highly strategic and easily understood what rewards meant. Second, she had some basic motives—most notably food—that made it easy to give her high-motive rewards. Put simply, she was her father's child.

Our son possessed neither of these qualities. He was not strategic and hardly had a self-interested bone in his body. He didn't care about much that was material. For him, toilet training was something that was going to please us, and for that reason he was interested. Read him a book and he would stay on the potty. The attention was enough. This all seemed to suggest that we might be able to get results for a song.

Nonetheless, there was very little progress. So we decided to implement the more explicit incentive system, which had worked (kind of) well with Child No. 1. But there was a twist:

Child No. 1 was now around, and in many ways, we needed her help. She could easily detract from our efforts if not fully on board.

So the new plan became this: Child No. 2 would receive a sweet reward—one or two jelly babies, as the case may be. But also, whenever he was successful, Child No. 1 would receive the same. We viewed this as a team effort, and Child No. 1 was part of the team. To align her incentives we gave her a share of the pie.

That part worked swimmingly. She encouraged our son to sit on the potty and spent time showing him books. It seemed that we may have efficiently outsourced this activity: something valuable in our time-strapped lives.

Alas, it was not quite to be. We had to put a stop to it all when we discovered Child No. 1 feeding Child No. 2 copious amounts of water to help the process along! (By the way, in case you're wondering, Child No. 1 was four years old at the time.)

Nothing seemed to work with Child No. 2, and a deadline was looming. He was about to turn three and could go to preschool so long as he was toilet trained. Three weeks away from his birthday, we were desperate (Not just for us but for him. Preschool was much more fun than day care.)

So we established toilet training boot camp. The diapers were confiscated. The rugs were removed from our wooden floors, and we would do this as long as it took. He understood the basics but just needed intensive experience—so that is exactly what we provided.

Now you may think this sounds somewhat cruel. Well, I did some research, and apparently this was nothing compared with the methods of Nathan Azrin, whose book is tantalizingly entitled *Toilet Training in Less Than a Day*. This book, published in 1989, ranks in the top one thousand books sold even today. But if you read the reviews, the results are definitely mixed; even fans say the method takes a lot more than one day. I didn't buy the book, and we persisted with our methods; if we had to, we would come back to it as a last resort.

The first week was tough: he definitely wanted his diaper back, and we had to buy more floor cleaner. The second week was more successful—100 percent results on number twos but still some problems with number ones. We were getting close. Then, in the final week, he got it.

We turned up to the preschool and announced our success. They then told us that training pants would have been just fine. So much for rules. Sigh.

In the end, it was the attention and intensive experience that did it, but all this indicates something else, too: it will happen when it happens.

Sadly, we were not done yet. Incentives came back in force when we moved on to night training. I'll take a breath and recount that can of worms next.

Night training is a particularly difficult business. Your child has the day down pat, but at night, they might be asleep or too drowsy to know the signs. That means a period of time when they wear diapers or training pants at night. For parents, success begins when these are dry in the morning, and the training is complete when they are dry for a week or more.

In relation to Child No. 1, our philosophy was: what doesn't go in, doesn't come out. Her bed time was 6:30, so for two hours prior to that she was mostly off fluids. This wasn't a conscious plan, and we fell upon it by accident. But it worked, and we achieved official night training. (Actually, it turns out that we were just lucky. Whatever chemical processes needed to work did work, and the routine of before and after bed seemed to stick.)

We were not so lucky with Child No. 2. For starters, he got thirsty, and it is not advisable to deny a child water. But also, the concepts didn't quite click. He didn't seem too bothered about the whole thing, and we noticed that he would get up dry, claim he didn't need to go to the toilet, and then go in his diaper; or later, his training pants. This smelled (literally) of the basis of an incentive problem: once again, his interests were not aligned with ours.

Training pants have little pictures that disappear if "accidents" occur. This gave us a visible and external monitoring device. It was viewable both to us and our son. So that is the first thing we would check in the morning, and a celebration would ensue if the pictures were still there.

As you can guess, celebrations only get you so far. So, as has been our pattern throughout all of this, we moved to more tangible rewards. He was old enough to understand a points system that would lead to rewards. So a dry night would get a point, and seven points would get you a reward—usually a book or a toy. This was sufficient motivation, and he had a clear focus: "Make sure the pictures don't go out and you get a point."

Well we had some good nights and intermittent accidents. But then we had a full week of dry training pants. Much rejoicing ensued, including a bonus; no more training pants. Sadly, the next night there was an accident. "These things happen," you might say. But it turns out, the problem was that these things hadn't happened.

Our son had a small rubbish bin in his room. Upon inspection, we found five full training pants. Child No. 2 was getting up in the morning, noticing the pictures were gone, and getting himself a new pair of training pants! There was nothing malicious in this. He just understood the rule as: "Produce training pants with pictures." And so he worked out how to do just that.

Once more the old adage "you get what you pay for" was raising its ugly head. We paid for dry training pants, so that is what we got.

Our response was to impose a new requirement: you must have the same training pants on in the morning as you did in the night. It was easy to monitor, and we did.

We got a couple of nights of success, and then one morning I went into his room and found his bed wet. His training pants were dry. I asked him about this and he said, "It just happened."

"But how? It should have wet your training pants."

"No it wouldn't. I didn't have them on. They were on the night stand."

It turned out that Child No. 2 had been removing his training pants to ensure they were dry in the morning! I guess that worked. And we didn't notice because the relevant part of his body was concealed under the covers.

When it comes down to it, giving children incentives is a bit like programming a computer. Unless you get the instructions just right, problems can ensue. There is an episode of *Star Trek: The Next Generation* where Geordi programs the holodeck for a game "that could defeat Data" (the android) and ended up creating a sentient program that almost destroyed the *Enterprise*. Programming our son posed the same challenges.

We focused on the pictures on the training pants, so that is where our son placed his considerable creative energy. What we needed was a "program" that gave exactly what we wanted: no accidents. That is what we turned to after that night. It took some months, but eventually we were successful. We moved our focus away from the training pants (although getting rid of them became a common incentive as he grew older) and onto the behavior, which is what we really cared about.

So, just as we found with Child No. 1, incentives can work—but sometimes they work too well. So much care and management is required.

Finally, after eight-and-a-half years of this, we arrived at Child No. 3. And what had we learned? We'd realized that we were not equipped for the job—so we acted accordingly. We adopted a strategy, ruthlessly efficient in its application and very light in terms of taxing our own energy: we *outsourced* the whole deal.

Now, by outsourcing, I don't mean that we just sent our daughter away to some service and then they delivered her back to us, ready to go. Apparently those do exist for dogs, and I won't gloss over the fact that we wouldn't have availed ourselves of a human service had it existed. But it does not.[3] Instead, we relied on her day care providers to handle the entire exercise. They initiated toilet training, encouraged our daughter and eventually succeeded, well before we did much at all at home. All we were left to do was to set her straight at home which, suffice to say, was not too hard once she had revealed her abilities to the wider community.

Day care is the perfect place for all this. First of all, the providers have as much, if not more, incentive as we do to get children trained. They change more diapers and also have to potentially deal with the children for years to come. They have no desire for a "slow to train" child. Of course, our son had to leave their capable hands before he was done and move to a preschool that required a trained kid. That dampened incentives somewhat. But give day care providers a future with another thousand diaper changes and we have a tight alignment of interests.

Second, and this goes without saying, they have seen it all. They are simply more capable in terms of knowing the signs, assessing readiness, and doing all of the other crap (literally) that first-time parents think about but cannot do.

Finally, the children have peers at day care. Now the power of peer pressure is something that can lead to both good and evil. The evil usually becomes apparent when your child follows others to leap off a several-feet-high structure or starts sucking noodles up their nose. But the good can be equally powerful. If all the other kids are successfully going to the toilet, there is intense pressure to join in, and to do so in a meaningful way. Your child wants to get the same cheers their friends are getting for demonstrating this activity. And they don't want to be tended to for a soiled diaper.

Even wearing a diaper can be socially difficult. A friend's three-year-old son, who didn't attend day care, shed his diaper himself when a random older kid made fun of him in a playground. Of course, that meant no nighttime diaper either and a few difficulties for his parents as a result of that.

But our daughter gave up diapers at day care. Indeed, in the early days, she would convince some of the more part-time workers that she didn't wear a diaper; although apparently those earlier forays met with unfortunate results. But it continued later on, too. I remember being informed, after having collected her and driven halfway home, "I don't need to wear a diaper!" Turned out she was diaper free. Being on the freeway, there was not much I could do. So I went with it, and it turned out, thankfully, that she was correct.

I won't pretend that we were totally free of obligation. For a while, there was a distinct difference between her behavior at home and elsewhere. But once we got on the program and deployed a few incentives, we had complete success in a matter of days.

So the moral of our story is simple. When you come across (virtually) one-time activities that you have no competence to manage, you should outsource them to those who deal with these things regularly and who also have plenty of experience. The end result is mostly the same as if you did it yourself, but with less stress and much cleaner carpets.

PART III

THE LOGISTICS

6 Cleaning

There comes a time in every parent's life when they have to cast aside the idea of their child as a little baby, dependent on them for everything. For me, that time came when I stepped on a Lego brick with bare feet. There are few things quite as painful—although this is mostly because of the unexpected shock of it. "Would you please put this stuff away!" I exclaimed, only to be greeted by fluttering eyelids and a toothy smile, as if to say, "Are you talking to me? Your baby?"

Various acts of cleanliness are perhaps the first things we parents expect our children to do by themselves. From cleaning up toys and washing hands to not "mistaking" sleeves for handkerchiefs, we hope our children will do all these things at a very young age.

Indeed, I think this is why we read them *The Cat in the Hat* (and its sequel) so frequently—books that supply the ultimate in role empathy. The children are left alone, and then the cat comes in and makes a terrible mess. Panic ensues, but the cat doesn't just leave everything to the others, he deals with the mess all by himself. This is what we aspire to: if you do make a mess, deal with it. "Should we tell her about it?" Frankly, we don't care, it's the results that matter.

Yet it is a constant struggle. While hygiene is something you can tie back to health, with general mess you don't have the same moral authority. And while mess is easy to see, germs are somewhat imaginary from a child's perspective, so explaining what you want and what "success" is can be a challenge. Your goal is to move things to a point where you can trust your kids. But they realize very quickly that the path to trust is littered with work. Conflict ensues.

One way to deal with such conflicts is, of course, by using various sticks and carrots. We employ them regularly, with a healthy dose of shouting on the side. But there is not much here that isn't endemic to all situations where some punishment or encouragement is warranted. Moreover, these devices, especially with smaller children, do not work too well.

One reason, of course, is that parents are generally in a weak bargaining position. Every child seems to know that it will take more time for a parent to negotiate with them over cleaning up than it would just to do it themselves. All they have to do is hold out a little, and the free service they've enjoyed in the past will continue unabated.

So with the lack of aligned interests, the primary issue with cleaning is the sheer logistics of it all. How do you organize your lives so that basic hygiene is maintained, and if it isn't, you know about it? How do you manage the mess so that it doesn't get out of control? And how do you avoid the pain associated with hard plastic in the heel? And then what do you do when an infestation invades the household and some drastic action is required?

Here is a simple request: "When you go to the bathroom, please wash your hands with soap before coming out." The reason is obvious to adults. It has been scientifically proven that this will reduce the spread of germs, and so everyone, including you, will be somewhat healthier as a result.

The compelling nature of this argument can easily be lost on a child, so they need constant reminders and attention as they learn to carry out this simple hygienic task. Now, if you thought that this was because an understanding of the science of microbiology was required, you would be mistaken. When you take a group of people who definitely understand the science and the consequences, you don't get much better behavior. It turns out that there is a constant struggle to get doctors—yes, medical professionals—to wash their hands.

According to an Australian study, on average doctors believed they washed their hands 73 percent of the time, but some close monitoring revealed that this only happened 9 percent of the time.[1] And this was in a pediatric intensive care unit! In my experience, children are less delusional.

Hospitals try all sorts of measures to get doctors to wash their hands, including providing alcohol-based disinfectants so that they don't have to search for a sink. But this isn't enough. Neither is monitoring, an array of motivational posters, or arming wardens with disinfectants to be applied in the car park as doctors arrive at work.[2] Even handing out coffee vouchers to compliant doctors gives no appreciable results. As a parent, you have to ask, if they can't get doctors to wash their hands, how on earth will we get our children to do so?

In our household, hand washing is an activity of high importance; certainly more so than before we had children. Before and after any child has any meal (defined here as any bit of food), hand washing occurs. The before is for the bacteria. The after is for the furniture.

Our system involves extensive monitoring—especially for Child No. 2. He is at an age (six) where he has a high need for washing and a low inclination. So we have to engage in a comprehensive system of auditing—that is, hand smelling. Contrast this with our youngest (three). She is a sucker for routine and has (for the moment at least) adopted hand washing as a regular part of life; so much so that she often assists us as the enforcer. Indeed, she often reminds her parents (mostly me), exhibiting her future dictatorial tendencies.

But all this is costly. We have to monitor all of the time, without the extensive administrative resources of a hospital. What we would like to do is trust our children to carry out this activity. The same situation was, of course, a more serious dilemma for hospitals and doctors. One solution they found was to take doctors' hands and scan them to show how much crap was on them. Providing data was the key. They even posted the scans on screen savers. The result was 100 percent compliance. Data plus shame equals trust.

This type of scanning machine would work well in our household. Imagine having to put your hands on some device that would give you a hand rating. While children may not understand the consequences, they could certainly be taught to understand the rating. If you kept doing this, they'd become nicely obsessively compulsive about not doing anything without a "green" (or whatever) rating, and good habits would be formed.

Now if some entrepreneur wanted to develop a scanner for other settings, I am sure that as the technology was refined, it would find a decent home and school market too.

Hygiene is a relatively black-and-white issue. It is hard to argue against it morally even if there is a general compliance problem. But when it comes to everyday mess—you know, disorganization in the form of stuff strewn all over the floor—passions can be ignited. In our household, we engage in a war on mess that occupies considerable resources and meets with a similar level of resistance and protest.

There is a distinct ideological element to the war on mess. According to a somewhat subversive *New York Times* article, provocatively entitled, "Saying yes to mess,"[3] there are those who have abandoned the fight. Indeed, they have come back with a new ideology, proudly advocating that mess is, in fact, a good thing; spurring an "anti-anticlutter movement." This is based on various studies that demonstrate that desks in an apparent state of disorder lead to more creative and better-paid careers, and that more relaxed and competent moms and dads aren't too fussy in the closet-cleaning department. The article described the ideology as reassuring us that "really neat people are not avatars of the good life; they are humorless and inflexible prigs, and have way too much time on their hands." Now I am happy to accept that there are lots of points of view: but let's face it, this is extremist propaganda. It simply can't be true that a free-for-all on mess would be a good thing. However, it does help us focus on the real question: *What is the optimal amount of mess?*

This question, when considered for households with children, has some special features. This is not only because children have their own "values" on the subject, but also because parents make conscious attempts to mold those values. Moreover, like many issues, it is the existence of children that forces many adults to consider their own values on this subject closely and in some cases take a definitive stance on mess. This is especially the case since some mess (say, small objects) can be potentially fatal to small children.

In some households, the desired amount of mess is zero. And such houses do actually exist—I have seen them. They appear to be clutter free all of the time, and the children are clutter free too. They sit and read books and such. They look sterile and usually have expressions to match. It is quite a picture.

I'll call these folks "up-wingers." They like to put everything away, up in closets, on shelves, and in attics. But, most significantly, their stuff is up off the ground.

To be truthful, part of me looks at up-wing households with wistful appreciation and envy. But then the rest of me perks up and thinks about the sheer energy that must be involved in getting to that point. So, for us, zero mess isn't a practical optimum. I am happy to obscure my unwillingness to expend effort under the guise of an ideological rationale—that the children would be oppressed by such a clutter-free life.

But what the *New York Times* article describes is the other extreme. Consider the view of Manhattan Rabbi Irwin Kula, who argues that "order can be profane and life-diminishing." He holds up his fifteen-year-old daughter's bedroom, with piles of clothes, photos, and junk on the floor, as "an invitation . . . to search for a deeper meaning under the scurf." Deeper meaning, my foot! It is only deeper because the floor has been raised by successive layers of mess. These are radical "down-wingers." Everything is down on the floor, on desks, and on kitchen counters.

We are not in this category. Indeed, I have a simple test as to whether your optimal amount of mess is less than this extreme. When you witnessed the events of 9/11, apart from everything else, did it ever occur to you: "What a mess! How are they ever going to clean that up?" And I don't mean the problem of terrorism but literally the physical mess it created right there at ground zero. If you had that thought sometime in the first day, you are not a mess extremist but a moderate; at least ideologically.

So our household has definite up-wing leanings, but not in an extreme way. However, I can't say that we've reached an ideological consensus on how to manage mess. The children's mother is a short-term up-winger; I am more in the long-term category.

To explain this, consider that much of this book has used the tools of microeconomics and applied them in the household. For mess management, however, the issues are more aligned with macroeconomics. It is not the pieces that make up a mess that are the issue, but rather the total amount of mess at any one time. And when we think of aggregate stuff like that, we can turn to the tools of macroeconomics for guidance.

The big issue in macroeconomics is how to manage the business cycle. This is the ebb and flow of economic life. Some years the economy is in a recession, and in others it climbs into a boom. So it is with mess. Mess is not a constant. It goes up, and it goes down. And as with macroeconomics, the goal is to smooth out the bad times, where there is an oversupply of mess, and expand the length of the good times. The question is, how much active intervention do you need to achieve this?

A good example of the mess cycle, and my attitude toward it, is what happens on the desk in my office. That desk starts perfectly clutter free and slowly accumulates paper until it reaches about a foot and a half high. Then I spend a day (every three months or so) "excavating." Excavating is the right word as I uncover layers of work that was done or, worse, should have been done. The deeper I go, the longer since it was laid down. You could measure time using mess in much the same way that geologists do using rock formations.

But here is where the differences in our household arise: I am happy to tolerate a longer period of mess than the children's mother. A week or more is fine by me. As for her, she likes to close off mess for the day in much the same way that a bond trader closes off their position overnight. That means a mess-free house to wake up to in the morning.

Given her preferences, she prefers to deal with mess as a constant war, with constant effort and vigilance. Not me. I prefer to look for structural solutions. Can we spend some money on something that will alleviate a mess issue for good?

A good example of this is what happened to the aptly named "pile of death" in our household. The pile of death was created and is maintained by the children's mother. It is where all of the correspondence and paper we get, and potentially have to deal with, goes. Birthday invites, catalogs, some bills, court summonses, and lots of other stuff goes there. It accumulates as a single pile on a desk near our kitchen. Everyone knows that if something gets put in the pile of death it will never be seen again. If the children see us putting an invitation into that pile they scream "Nooo! Not there!" They know their social life is doomed.

The problem with the pile of death is that it is unstable. When it reaches a certain height, gravity eventually takes over, bringing it all to the ground and creating a large mess. At that stage we come to the realization that nothing in the resulting mess is, in fact, useful anymore. The correspondence is then summarily transferred to the trash.

To eventually resolve this cycle, I invested in a set of small drawers, the sort peddled by anticlutter entrepreneurs. These drawers would house three categories of the pile of death: (a) current action, (b) on hold, and (c) the rest. This would enable some sorting and also the hope of finding something important we thought might be there, by looking in drawers (a) and (b). Gone were the mess and the clutter. And action was taken whenever a drawer became full. The kids have affectionately named these the "drawers of death."

My point is that the investment allowed us to deal with the mess itself and minimize effort and fuss. This, to me, is the only way to deal with "structural" as opposed to "frictional" mess. This is the fundamental trade-off in mess management. You have to choose between frictional solutions that involve day-to-day mess management and structural solutions that try to prolong mess periodicity. But how do you measure the degree of structural mess (as opposed to daily frictional mess)?

My metric is simple: time to clean up. How long would it take you to get all the clutter away? In some situations, this could take forever. You may find there is no feasible way to get all the clutter out of sight in your household. In other houses, it can be done, but this is no guarantee that it can be done usefully. So there is a sense in which the benchmark state of "no mess" has its shades of gray. But some households can be clutter free in ten minutes.

It is to this standard that we try to hold our children. This means that (a) there are restrictions on the total quantum of permissible mess, and (b) there are various ways of putting stuff away. The latter comprises boxes and other solutions from anticlutter peddlers such as IKEA. Our six-year-old son has embraced these. His solution was cupboards full of toys all neatly sorted in separate boxes. Using this system, he can clean his room in ten minutes even if every single toy is out, which happens regularly.

Child No. 1, on the other hand, despite being offered similar solutions, cannot manage her mess this way. She simply has too much stuff. So she makes sure she keeps the quantum down.

But even this is not enough. Children accumulate mess potential at a constant rate per annum. This means that we have to do a yearly cull. Get rid of all the stuff they have grown out of, don't use, or don't care about. Our son is quite cooperative and objectively handles this situation by ranking his stuff to go. For Child No. 1, there is no such thing as mere stuff she doesn't potentially need. She can construct a case to save every last thing from eviction—for example:

"What's this?"

"It is the lid from a pen."

"Why do you need it?"

"In case I find the pen."

"Didn't we throw out the pen last year because it had no lid?"

"No, that was another pen. I can also use the lid as a small cup."

And on it goes, item after item. Her life will be a constant struggle against the tide of accumulation of stuff. Hopefully our house can hold together until she moves out.

There comes a time when issues of cleaning reach a crisis. The whole household has to be mobilized against a threat that overtakes all other concerns. This happened to us when lice invaded. We had to engage in a large dose of nit-picking, getting down to the nitty-gritty and going over everything with a fine-toothed comb. It was a lousy situation and involved lots of activities that made us feel like nitwits.

Basically, we were at an event horizon where common sayings became literal. The previous paragraph was awash with five of these (can you pick them out?), all referring to our war on lice, as they were originally intended. I noticed this connection as we dealt with the situation. It turns out it is no accident.

> A number of common sayings actually refer to lice. Calling someone a "nitwit" is the same as saying they have the intelligence of a louse egg (nit). "Getting down to the nitty-gritty" and "nit-picking" refer to the detailed work involved in removing nits. Describing someone as "lousy" implies that they have lice.[4]

I can only suggest that, from our experience, these sayings deserve their common origin.

Lots of things happen when a family goes into a cleaning crisis like this. The first is the easy blame game. In our case, the finger was pointed squarely at Child No. 3 (two years old at the time) whose share of lice and lice eggs was 95 percent of the total in the house. She was constantly reminded of her crimes. But, in actuality, the real problem was that her share was not 100 percent.

When it comes down to it, children with lice are actually not the thing most parents fear. Instead, it is the thought of lice spreading to them. In our case, it was the children's mother who took the rest of the share of lice. That nightmare scenario meant she was going to have to trust someone else—namely, me—to deal with it. Head shaving was apparently a more viable and trustworthy option.

Lice are just one of those things that happen when your children play with other children. All the literature says they're just part of growing up and interacting socially. But it has occurred to us, more than once, that social interaction is overrated.

Lice can supposedly be treated within a day. In reality, a lice-free ring of confidence requires weeks of action. It takes plenty of time and patience, which, as you know, are in abundance in households with small children! First you need to kill the lice with some insecticidal hair foam. Then—and this is the fine-toothed comb bit—you must carefully brush each hair *individually*, applying liberal amounts of conditioner. We each went through this.

The conversations went something like this:

"Ow, you're pulling."

"I'm just trying to get through these knots to the scalp. And if you would stop moving your head and look down, that would help."

"But I can't see the TV."

"Well, I need to be able to see. Now just sit tight and behave yourself."

"I want to do something else. How much longer will it be?"

"It'll be over when it's over. Look, we have to do this. Don't you want to go to work tomorrow? If I don't do it properly, we'll be back here again. Do you really want that?"

"No, I guess not."

And this went on for several weeks before we were confident the infestation had been expunged.

On the brighter side, if you can imagine one, we did get to bring out the kids' microscope. That proved surprisingly useful. For starters, lice and their eggs can be small. This allowed us to identify them, their age, and whether they had hatched. The latter allowed us to rule out more aggressive treatment on one of us. I highly recommend your own lab work if you ever encounter this situation. It turned the whole exercise into a great learning opportunity.

Of course, all this made me wonder why there isn't some squad listed in the Yellow Pages who can come in and take care of the problem for you. Let's face it, there are surely gains to be made from becoming an expert here. I guess it probably has something to do with cross-contamination. But then again, this would be an issue with any medical service.

At some point, mess is created on such a scale that a decisive and major reaction is required—the kind of mess that the Cat in the Hat would be proud of. In some households, this happens when the children decide to cook for themselves and fail to distinguish between carpet and cooking surfaces. In others, it occurs when the outside is brought inside, usually in the form of mud, dead animals, or worse. For us, it was wall art.

One evening we had put Child No. 2, who was five at the time, to bed. Three hours later we came in, as we always did, to check on him. The scene that greeted us will be etched into our memory forever—and not just because we later took pictures.

The lights were on, and all over the walls of his room were drawings. There weren't just scribbles around where children can normally reach. Every area of exposed wall had an intricate set of pictures. Most of them involved stairs from various angles, with all sorts of people and animals parading up and down them. Other places had similar scenes of action. Even the light switch didn't escape; a little person was there turning it on and off.

Our son stood in front of us as we screamed in horror. "I didn't know. I didn't do it," he pleaded with dripping pen in hand. His eyes were bloodshot, and he had clearly been working all that time. We put Michelangelo to bed and dealt with him in the morning. He was left in no doubt that a repeat action would result in unprecedented punishment. I can't remember what his sentence was for this crime, but whatever it was, it was effective; nothing like that has ever happened again.

That left us with a large cleanup job, and it was too difficult for Child No. 2 to be able to help. When we talked about this, people wondered why we removed it all. After all, every other paper-based piece of art is kept, and, even we had to admit, this was an impressive piece of work. But we spent hours slowly expunging it from the room. To leave it there would be to legitimize the activity. To me, it would have meant that the terrorists had won the war on mess.

7 Traveling

The best thing you can say about traveling with children is that they are worse than baggage. Baggage can be hauled around and has no expectation of being treated well. If it gets lost it is a pain but not a disaster. Children, on the other hand, are baggage with mouths and legs. The mouths let their feelings be known, while the legs give them the ability to get lost without the assistance of airline handlers.

The most surprising thing about traveling with children, however, is how poorly various travel businesses—in particular, airlines—cater to them. Yes, it is true that some of the better airlines throw activity packs at children, while some long-haul flights have kids' movies and games. But entertainment is relatively easy for parents to deal with themselves. It is the rest of the experience that looms large; especially in relation to food. Food permeates the travel experience. Access to it and the ability to administer it effectively and cleanly are what separate the good from the bad travel experiences.

Delays, missed connections, and being lost are all tolerable so long as food is on hand. Consider the following story recounted by futurologist David Houle after he was stuck on the tarmac in Chicago:[1]

> We had now been on the plane for three hours, and since it was dinnertime, stomachs were growling and tempers were getting short. Then something unique happened. A flight attendant came on the intercom and said: "The very generous people sitting in 5D and 5E work for the Dove chocolate company and would like everyone to know that they would be glad to distribute candy bars to everyone on board. The choice is dark chocolate or milk chocolate with almonds." The applause and cheering was lusty, loud, and long. Food! Chocolate no less! A spontaneous act of human generosity and kindness for every passenger! The flight attendants then passed out large Dove chocolate bars asking "Dark chocolate or milk chocolate with almonds?" The mood on the plane was instantly infused with a bit of human magic and fun. Another prolonged round of applause broke out.

So let me get this straight. After more than three hours of frustrating delay, someone can just spontaneously give everyone a little chocolate to turn the whole event into an emotional outpouring and the basis of fond memories. It was cheap but regarded as one of the greatest gifts ever bestowed. So why can't travel businesses get their act together and focus on food; especially when there are children involved?

Actually, not all aspects of travel lead to food issues. By choosing the right destination, many options present themselves.

What is curious are the schemes resorts and hotels employ to cater to children on the ground.

At one of the places we regularly go on family vacations, we are attracted by the policy that kids "stay free and eat free." Now, "stay free" is really a slogan in name only. It means they won't charge you for your kids if you can stuff them into your room. Obviously, there are considerable minuses with doing that, so you end up paying for larger accommodation and nonfree stays.

But "eat free" is another matter. Child No. 1, as I have mentioned before, really likes to eat. We hear howls of complaint if a third course isn't forthcoming. So if she could eat free, surely that would be an advantage to us.

Well, not quite. For starters, one might have assumed that if you went to a restaurant where the kids ate free, the portions for them would be small. Not so. They are on the larger side of meals I have seen for kids and usually include dessert. But here is the thing. If I thought that we would be receiving a massive subsidy from the families with kids who ate an average amount, I was gravely mistaken. This is because those families still order the maximum amount of food for their kids, even if it doesn't get eaten. Yes, there is a social loss from this, but there is no implicit subsidy coming our way either.

So who is paying for the kids' meals? You would like to think it was the parents. Again, not quite. The restaurant might jack up prices for parents' meals or drinks, or somehow it could be built into the resort charges. Sadly, however, that can't be the case. As we ate our meal, I noticed plenty of tables free of kids. Those people were paying the same as us for the meal and, even if they were getting a discount on the resort charges, the meal itself was a worse deal for them.

A natural thing to ask, however, is what were those people doing there? The resort has plenty of other restaurants that are not part of the "kids eat free" deal. All they'd have to do is avoid us to get a better deal. But the problem is this: those other restaurants cannot be cheaper, in terms of price at least. If they were, then savvy parents might decide that it would be worthwhile paying for the kids—especially if, unlike us, they could get away with feeding their kids very little.

What this means is that to confine the families with kids to the kid-designated restaurants, the "free of kids" restaurants have to be at least as expensive, if not more so, just to make sure. So, who is really paying for the "kids eat free" deal? Well, it's the adults without kids, who don't want to eat with someone else's! Our kids eat free so that someone else can eat free of kids and pay for it. I know this because on some evenings, we get a sitter. On those occasions, we go out free of kids and end up paying more.

One final little puzzle. As I note later in this chapter, airlines do not appear to think enough about mess when giving meals to children on planes. The same is true of the "kids eat free" restaurants. We went to a nice Chinese restaurant at the resort one night, and our daughter, who was two years old at the time, appeared to happily eat up all her fried rice. "Wow, she's doing well. This place is great." It was only after the meal, when she was removed from her high chair, that we saw how well she had done. There was a nice layer of rice over her, the chair, and the floor. Let me be clear, this was (mostly) a mess that the restaurant had to deal with.

But there is a clear alternative for them, and I do not understand why they don't exercise it. The alternative is takeout. As it was a Chinese restaurant, I observed plenty of people taking away food during our meal. I wondered whether we could still get the "kids eat free" deal if we did the same. But apparently not. One explanation was that they were trying to sell the adults more alcohol. Again, not so. Indeed, the whole operation is so efficient that you could be out of there in forty-five minutes (which is not conducive to the leisurely consumption of high-margin items).

Another possibility was that a takeout option would be subject to abuse (like ordering too many meals or something). Again, this is not necessarily true. Since all the customers were staying on site, it is not hard to imagine a simple voucher system that could be used to prevent abuse.

So I am left with the thought that they must require the kids to "eat free" on site because that will demonstrate to those adults who mistakenly happen upon these places one night that they should never do that again and should instead pay for the "free of kids" places. It is like the crammed seats in economy, which are there to show business class passengers why they should pay more. It is nice to see how our kids are pawns in the exercise of resort market power.

It is really in the air that food becomes a key issue for parents. This is not to say that airline travel involves an absence of food. Far from it. Indeed, the main activity for our children on planes is eating. All the other things one might try, from computer games to books, lack food's surefire attention-grabbing power. But there is one small problem: airlines do not know what the heck they are doing.

Let me explain. By far the most sensible option would seem to be preordering a child's meal for your child. A rational person would think that, in preparing such a meal, the airline would give careful attention to the general needs of children and parents and structure an offering that, while certainly not lavish, would cover all the bases and get the job done.

Well, throw rationality out the window, because here is what actually happens. Let's suppose that you end up getting the child's meal that you ordered—and this is a big suppose, because it might well not come, or worse, might come for one child but not the other. But say you actually get the child's meal; what's in it?

Here is the offering of a well-known Australian airline:

- One box of juice
- One muffin
- One fluorescent, sugary bar claiming to contain fruit
- One packet of corn flakes
- One cup of milk
- One fruit cup
- Cutlery, plastic of course
- One bowl
- One paper napkin

If that selection seems reasonable to you, then you are clouded by "ground-level" thinking. Here is what happens to this meal at a high altitude. First, child tries to insert little straw into box of juice. If successful, child, not understanding the subtleties of fluid dynamics, lightly squeezes box upon picking it up, causing juice, if you are lucky, to squirt in the child's face and, if you are not, to squirt over the child's head into the row behind. Very quickly that child is without juice—and remember, this was the first thing they reached for.

The child then asks for the bar, which is your cue to say, "How about eating something healthier first?" Why you say this in flight is beyond me. But you do. Then child goes for the muffin. However, only 30 percent of the muffin reaches their stomach. The rest forms a layer of crumbs over the child and the seat.

Still hungry, the child goes for the corn flakes, attempting to pull the lid off the milk cup—with predictable consequences. Some milk ends up in the bowl. More milk ends up in the child's lap, along with the muffin crumbs and the corn flakes that flew all over the place as, in this case, I tried to open that stupid little packet.

Ditto all this for the fruit cup, but substitute pieces of fruit for corn flakes and juice for milk.

Finally we get to the bar, which promptly sticks to the child's teeth. They complain. You then reach for the toothbrush you carry around for such emergencies. . . . OK, so you take your finger and attempt to scrape the fruit confection off their teeth but end up getting it all over your hands; now you have little option but to turn into a five-year-old yourself and just wipe them on the seat.

Let us understand precisely what has happened here. There are no winners. The child has not really gotten food. The parent has not been relieved of stress. And the airline has some serious cleaning to do, which will affect their turnaround time.

But just think, all this could so easily have been avoided. First, you could be on an airline that does not provide meals. That forces you to find your own solutions, which would basically involve jelly babies (clean, sugary fun). Second, you may not order the child's meal, in which case an adult meal comes, and the child refuses to eat. The child is hungry (just as with the child's meal), but things are cleaner.

Finally, the airline may give an ounce of thought and (a) supply juice in a pop-top plastic bottle rather than a box and straw; (b) provide a cookie that doesn't leave too many crumbs; and (c) include some fresh fruit, such as grapes. Why not top it all off with a little toy, like McDonald's does? Then we'd all be happy.

Of course, at the other end of the flying spectrum is the "low-cost" airline route. There you have no expectations of being given food. Instead what you hope is that you will be charged through the roof for something.

Before we come to that, the low-cost route has another issue when you travel with kids—getting a seat. In many such flights, there is no assigned seating. Now I can imagine a world in which no assigned seating might make sense. If there is a commuter flight with mostly lone travelers, they would get on the plane and sit in the nearest available seat. It probably means that you can load people on quicker.

But for a flight to a vacation destination, with mostly families traveling, the whole thing is a disaster. There is no appreciable saving in time, because the large chunks of families scramble to get seats close to their children. Now I had fantasized about not doing this; going to the back of the queue and being separated from our children for the whole flight, leaving them as some other sap's problem. Sadly, the issue is that, as in musical chairs, I would likely end up sitting next to someone else's children—and that was a lottery I was not willing to play.

Anyhow, on our one and only experience with this, we had a "prized" orange pass, which meant that we would be first to board—being with kids got us that. It was clearly better than the blue pass or, worse, something called the silver pass (I do not know who you would have had to offend to get stuck with one of those). But you may have noticed my earlier foreboding. The "prized" orange pass was only prized in the sense that there were a couple of people with the other passes. Actually, from a scarcity (but no value) perspective, the other passes were rarer.

I was not really aware of this, and we had positioned ourselves well to get on the flight at the head of the queue. Unfortunately, fifteen minutes before boarding, owing to one of our adult party being in the bathroom, I watched the "tipping point" occur. It occurred to someone that they could just stand in line right then, and they did. Within seconds, as if someone shouted "fire" in a cinema, there was a rush to the queues. I thought the worst that might happen would be that we were at the back of the prized orange queue. In dismay I now saw that the orange queue accounted for more than half the passengers! Nonetheless, we stood in it.

Fifteen minutes into standing in this queue, Child No. 1, who was seven at the time, asked, "Why are we just standing here?" I told her that it was because of the "tragedy of the queue." Everyone wanted to be at the front of the queue, so we all moved to get there. "But we aren't in the front of the queue," she said, pointing out the obvious. Well, we weren't quite at the back either. We were standing there so we wouldn't be at the back. "And what's the problem with being at the back?" I argued that it was because we wanted a better choice of seats.

Now we had become savvy enough to realize that there was another opportunity to jump the queue, as we walked across the tarmac to the plane. We weren't going to do this, but we were certainly going to maintain our relative position against the "blue passers" nipping at our heels, unencumbered by children. One got through, but we broadly succeeded.

On the plane, the true inefficiency of this system emerged. People who boarded at the front were going back. People who boarded at the back were going forward. They collided. It was chaos. We staked out our row and wanted to maintain a spare seat. (There were only eight on the flight.) Fortunately, Child No. 3 put on a wonderful screaming performance and repelled all challengers.

Being seated, we could then contemplate the food situation. We had intended to buy food on the plane, to save the hassle of carrying it on with us. Big mistake. We were in the middle of the plane and by the time the food cart got to us, there was no food. Certainly no real food, like sandwiches or meat pies. We got some potato chips and a bag of candy. Now you might think our flight was outside of mealtime, but no, it was the prime time 12–3 p.m. run. Lunchtime. Hence the high demand for food, but that didn't explain the low supply.

Then I had an idea. I would try to procure a sandwich from the row ahead. I said, "I'll give you $15 for your sandwich." The woman I was negotiating with pondered this and then said "how about $30?" I said, "$20?" She said, "No deal." I said, "Are you really going to eat a sandwich that is now worth $20 in cold hard cash?"

Actually, the last paragraph didn't happen, but pondering the potential for it left me with that strong memory. I also wanted to remember to bring more contraband onto the next such flight I had the misfortune to travel on. I think I could make a killing.

While food can relieve much of the stress associated with travel, it is useful to reflect on the ultimate source of that stress: other passengers. I don't mean that they actively cause problems. Instead, it is their very existence and the general desire by parents to be considerate of them in confined conditions that generates stress. You might not personally care that your child is being loud, mobile, or messy, except for the fact that this so immediately impacts on others who have no obvious avenue of escape on a full flight.

But what happens when they can escape? My belief is that all bets are off in the consideration game. This happened to us once when we were traveling with just two children—Children No. 1 and 2, when they were aged three and one respectively.

The flight in question was about two hours long and fairly—but not completely—full. An enterprising agent at check-in had offered us the strategic option of two aisle seats either side of a center seat that we did not book. At that time, children under three generally sat on their parents' laps to travel. The agent figured that this seating arrangement would virtually guarantee a vacant seat between us, so we could use the extra space.

Sadly, the inevitable happened; someone was assigned the center seat. He was a man in his twenties who had bought his ticket at the last minute. He was the last person to board. The flight attendant immediately offered him a seat farther back, which he refused. This frustrated the flight attendant, but we didn't seem to have any other option, so I scooted over and gave him one of the aisle seats. I figured the other seats were too far back for him.

After takeoff, I got up and noticed that there was an empty middle seat just three rows back. This was the one this guy had refused, presumably in the hope I would do just what I had done and give him the aisle. Sure, we had been strategic, but I was still outraged. Now I understood the flight attendant's frustration at his earlier intransigence. The weight of travel stress was suddenly lifted from my shoulders. I decided that I was going to torture this man for as long as he stayed in my domain.

My first act was to take out the air sickness bag and say to the three-year-old sitting on my lap, "OK, now we don't want to have a repeat of what happened last time, do we? Here's the bag, right here. If you're feeling sick you need to get it so that you don't throw up over the nice man here." Child No. 1, who had never thrown up on a flight before, took some interest in the air sickness bag but dutifully agreed to use it should she need to. She also obliged me by having a loud discussion about what being sick on an airline meant, in all of the gruesome detail that can accompany three-year-old expressiveness.

The man looked nervous at this but was unmoved. I now gave Child No. 1 free reign to play as she wished, making no attempt to stop her bothering our fellow passenger. This amused me for some time, but it wasn't enough. I wanted more.

Next up I swapped the three-year-old for the one-year-old and decided to feed him some lunch. I seated him on my lap facing the increasingly disconcerted man and started spooning his pureed meal into his mouth—pretty poorly, too. He finally saw the writing on the wall and disappeared. I did not see him again until he returned at the very end of the flight.

It was the least stressful plane trip I have ever had with kids. When you take away the need to be considerate to others, air travel becomes a bearable experience.

8 Caring

It takes two to tango, they say. And when a diaper has, to put it mildly, "lost containment," it also takes two to deal with the mess. One for the mess on the child; the other for the mess everywhere else. If you just have one person, chances are you will clean up the child only to find that the other mess spreads to them later. Alternatively, you will clean up the other mess only to find that your child has taken the insult farther.

As a two-parent family, we have extreme sympathy for one-parent households. We have empathy too, because more often than not, there is just one of us in the house. It just isn't the same, because we usually have a break. Indeed, I have often wondered whether two is enough. Just because two people happen to have made a child doesn't seem to me to necessarily imply that only those two people should care for it.

It is probably fair to say that, these days, we parents are not the only ones involved in caring for our children. There are extended families, day care, and, of course, machines. Yes, machines.

When we had our third child, we finally succumbed and bought one of those musical electronic rocker swings. Baby goes in, baby is amused looking at a mobile, then baby falls asleep. It frees up your hands and saves your mind. If your baby does not understand that you have things to do that are in their interest (washing, preparing food, going to the bathroom), this will convince them. It was wonderful. I could not believe that we had two children before discovering the joy of it.

Of course, the idea of machine or electronic babysitting, if taken too far, will probably not be a good way of caring for a child. But, in some circumstances, any guilt that might be in place should surely be removed.

Take, for instance, plane flights. If I had a dollar for how many times I have heard the following story . . .

> I thought we should get one of those portable LCD DVD players for the kids on the flight, but my partner was dead against it. I ended up buying it anyway, and we both now agree it is the best purchase we've ever made.

There are times when electronic babysitters appear to be a must-have. When we traveled with an infant, things were relatively easy. The baby was contained, and our only worry was that her noise would disturb others. As children get older, our chief fear is restlessness. Put simply, they have to sit in a chair for what to them is a record-breaking long time, and we are fooling ourselves if we believe we can sustain entertainment for them on any flight of longer duration than an hour.

There are troublesome ages for kids on flights—I'd say from the age of one until they're six or seven years old. After that, they can entertain themselves with a computer game or a book. But prior to that, we are left with the following options: (a) reading to them (max twenty minutes); (b) drawing (max fifteen minutes); and (c) eating (max twenty minutes, but fraught with danger). Let's add that up: fifty-five minutes. On a lucky flight, we get another ten minutes with the in-flight diaper change—including the five minutes while we negotiate incredible long-term concessions to get the other parent to do it.

The DVD player (or these days, an iPod) can fill the void. Even if a child can only be occupied for half-hour spurts, sandwiching these in between other activities can extend your range to three or four hours. After that, drugs can be used to induce sleep.

What is more, a DVD player for a child on a flight generates a positive externality. The passengers around us were much better off. Indeed, any traveler without children might like to consider carrying a DVD player just in case, as an option for misguided parents.

Like all things, there is a time and a place for an electronic babysitter. Blanket policies against ever using them may be self-defeating, and overturned before long. Handing a child over to the machine when the costs of not doing so are high seems like a no-brainer.

More often than not, machine-based care is inappropriate, especially for day-to-day stuff. But the thought of it doesn't seem as divisive as day care—that is, letting someone else take care of your kids outside of the house.

Hardly a month goes by without another study that hits the headlines on the positive or negative effects of day care. A recent, scientifically comprehensive study observed over a thousand children until the age of six.[1] This led to front-page stories on how day care causes unruly kids in school later on.

But what did the study actually show? The biggest single impact on children's behavior and development is, of course, what their parents happen to do. This was regardless of whether they were in day care or not. Next, it turned out that, if a child spent time in a higher quality day care (with higher worker-to-child ratios), things like their vocabulary were significantly better. And in terms of behavior, if a child spent one or two years before school in day care, there was no impact. But if they spent significantly longer and they were in a poorer quality day care environment, chances are their behavior in school later on would not be as good. This last result was picked up by the newspapers and used to smear day care in general.

Even these weak implications are undermined by the fact that children do not spend time in day care randomly. Their parents choose to send them there. And let's face it, if your child was at the more unruly end of the spectrum, you would be more likely to look for help in caring for them, and perhaps be willing to accept lower quality in the mix. In that case, it is unclear whether the day care or the child is causing the behavioral findings. My point here is that, like much of the science directed at understanding what is good for children, without random assignment we just don't know if practices actually cause outcomes or whether it's the other way around.[2]

The more interesting question is why these studies—regardless of how well they are conducted—always receive prominent news attention. My theory is that day care is a divisive issue because parents have made choices in this regard and will always seek to justify them. However, let me first declare my own biases and actions. First, the actions. All three of our children have been in day care from very young ages (ranging from two to six months depending on the child). They were in for three, four, or more days a week as they grew older. As to my beliefs regarding the impact of day care, my view is that it has been wonderful. The children are more social, engaged, and happy than they would have been had one of us stayed at home full time.

Now for my theory: your beliefs about how good or bad day care is have a one-to-one correspondence with the decision you have made. And so they should—one would expect nothing less than for you to base your decision on your beliefs. However, just like the findings in scientific studies, I also think that the causality can go back the other way. The fact that you have chosen one path or another also has a role in shaping your beliefs.

The reason is this: either decision is actually quite hard on a day-to-day basis. If you stay at home, you have a constant struggle. To maintain your sanity and also to justify forgoing your career, loss of income, and other factors, it really helps to believe in what you are doing at a moral level. If you send your child to day care, you have a different struggle. You miss your children and sometimes feel guilty about leaving them there. Again, to maintain your sanity, you justify this at a moral level. Staying at home would not be as good for the child. You could not provide them with the same learning experiences and social interactions, among other things.

Thus, for every day that you take one path over the other, you are investing in the moral righteousness of your decision. So when you encounter others who have made different choices, there is little common ground. Things get debated, and offense is easily created. Take this account from Emily Bazelon:[3]

> One day when my older son Eli was about 2, he charmed the woman ahead of us in line at the supermarket. They grinned and goo-goo-ed at each other, and then Eli's new friend turned to me with a big smile and said, "He must be at home with you." I stammered no and started babbling: Eli was in day care, but it was really wonderful day care, with only twelve kids and five teachers, and really if you visited him there you would see. . . . But the woman's smile had vanished. We stood in embarrassed silence until her groceries were bagged.

Not surprisingly, stratification and segmentation arises, and like tend to hang out with like.

Which brings me to the media interest in the science or otherwise of day care. One side or the other will consume a given piece of evidence voraciously and dismiss all the other findings. In either case, the science is used as a "consumption good" rather than an "information good."

Overwhelmingly, the scientific literature says there is little in the way of vast systematic differences in outcomes and that other things matter a lot more. This means that the vast differences in peoples' views on day care have no basis in reality. Chances are, whatever you are doing in this regard is good for your child, and if others are doing something different, that is no reflection on you. It's time to find a little common ground.

All that said, one situation where surely the idea of day care is uncontroversial is when you are left on your own. I am not talking about a few hours a day. That might not be much parenting fun, but it is manageable. However, when one parent goes away for an extended period, how much capacity you have to care for a child really comes out.

One day, the children's mother abandoned us. She went off for a week at a spa. The kids asked me, "Why?" Going with the truth, I said that she wanted to get away from us. "Hopefully, she'll be back. We will just have to wait and see."

Outsiders reacted in the usual manner: "So you're Mr. Mom this week?" Mr. Mom, indeed! I don't think so. They talked as if I had never done anything for the kids and would surely be unable to cope. I'll tell you that I have been there before—and for a four-year stretch too.

You see, we had our first two kids while their mother was studying part-time for her MBA. That took four long years. And during those years, I did everything (yes, including feeding the baby, but no, not carrying the unborn children). I did the cooking, washing, and other sundry activities, on top of working. So I'd cope for a week just fine.

I didn't expect any awards for this. It's just what you do. Although I should also tell you that on the day of her last exam for that MBA, I was fired. Yes, "fired" in the Donald Trump sense of the word. My services for most of these things were no longer required.

It turns out that I hadn't been doing a good enough job. It was adequate and, by any normal standard, exemplary. But, as you might have grasped from earlier chapters, that isn't the standard of aspiration in our household. It is a higher standard. For four long years, she silently steamed at my poor performance, knowing full well that she didn't have the time or energy to wrest any tasks from me. But it was all over when that MBA was done.

So the week she was away represented a move back to the past. Take, for example, the dishwasher. For the past four years, the philosophy has been that it can't handle the task itself. Instead, dishes need to be clean before they go in the washer. I have pointed out the environmental inefficiency of this. I have also engaged in the two obvious errors: I have put dirty dishes away, and I have put clean dishes on for another cycle. Quite frankly, it is hard to tell them apart.

Indeed, sometimes I rush to get a load on, get it done, and then put away before anyone finds out. But even then it is hard. I end up having to do more washing, because there is always that one tiny bit of food that doesn't come off but gets baked on. Then the finger is pointed squarely at you know who, and I have to apologize for thinking I could ever manage this task on my own.

Anyhow, during my sole-parent week, I could use the dishwasher how I wanted and cover for my own mistakes. So that is what happened.

But some other parenting things were not as easy for me this time as they were the first time around. A few weeks earlier, a hypothesis had emerged that our son's (sometimes) poor behavior might be the result of preservatives in his diet. I haven't read the science behind this. There was no point; he was put on a diet anyway. And let me tell you, I had no idea how many foods have preservatives in them.

Our son knows that sometimes he doesn't listen and do what he is told. With everyone else around him doing what they are supposed to, it has also concerned him. The preservatives hypothesis has freed him from responsibility for his actions, and he knows this. He happily tells me if he is not well behaved that perhaps there were some preservatives in his breakfast cereal, or that someone at school gave him something he shouldn't have eaten.

If he was more strategic, he might take this to another level and not keep me honest on his diet. Let me give him whatever so he would have free behavioral license. But no. He is a zealot to the cause, and so we are constrained in our eating habits.

This fact was not lost on Child No. 1, who is very strategic. Initially, she loved the diet because it satisfied her notion of fairness—no one should get more than her. So she would still get the same food while her brother's meal changed to, let's face it, a less appetizing variety. This was all to her liking, and so she embraced the diet theory.

But that was soon over. As the house was slowly cleared of all the food with preservatives, she realized that this was going to have an impact on her. Now, with the writing on the wall, she tried to move household opinion. She knew that while Mommy was away, there was a good chance of "party time."

Here's what she tried.

"It's unfair. Can't he just come to McDonald's and have a salad?" "Well, I don't know if those are sufficiently preservative free."

"Maybe we could go while he was somewhere else." "Well, that doesn't sound that fair."

"How do we know the preservatives were causing his bad behavior? He is not that well behaved now." "Well, it may take a while to work."

"But still, to be sure, we should reintroduce preservatives to his diet and then see if his behavior gets worse." "A randomized experiment, huh? Actually, that is pretty scientific. Maybe you can tell me how to work out if day care is good or not?"

Her brother was also happy to test the theory more conclusively. Child No. 1 pointed out to him that unless we experiment, he will never have anything good to eat again. On this basis, an insurgency brewed.

During the week, I came to find their arguments compelling; but the consequences of reversing the benefits of several weeks detoxifying with a single Happy Meal worried me. Sure, the theory might be wrong. But it could also be right. And the last thing I wanted was the responsibility for his poor behavior to be shifted from everything else to me. So, the regime held from afar. This is the kind of distance leadership a Roman emperor could have used.

By the end of the week, Child No. 1 had at last discovered a scientific way out of her brother's diet. One Saturday morning

I got up to find all three of them sitting at breakfast. The usual idea is that if they get themselves up, they can choose what they want to eat. Sadly, due to the constraints of my son's preservative-free diet, that didn't leave a lot of good options. However, apparently there was one thing they all knew was preservative free: the cooking chocolate. And so they simply substituted it for the usual cereal and had chocolate chips with milk. My daughter also put some "preservative-full" chocolate into her bowl and her younger sister's to test whether their behavior would get worse. Suffice it to say, there was going to be a heroic effort to make sure no one's behavior got worse! And as it turned out, they were all pretty well behaved—even during a trip to the supermarket, which is just asking for trouble.

So with the science over and after their mother had returned, we ended up, in part, able to free ourselves of the dietary explanations for the fact that my son sometimes doesn't listen to us. We went back to the reasons—that is, he is six, and he suffers from an older sister who is an extreme listener. (Hmm, perhaps she is preservative deficient?) Nonetheless, in the end our diet improved, but in a moderated rather than an extreme fashion. Also, some of our food is now going to last a bit longer in the pantry and fridge.

One thing that interests me about times like this—and this has happened every time the children's mother goes away—is the reaction of others. Put simply, most people treat me as if she has suddenly passed away. I get lots of:

"Oh I heard about that, how are you coping?" in a tone that suggests that the funeral was yesterday.

"Do the kids understand what has happened?" Yes, their Mommy has gone to a better place; a spa resort!

"What are you doing for food?" Well at the moment I have dangled the two-year-old outside as bait to see if we can catch something; it's what their mother would have wanted.

And so on. Fortunately, I expected her imminent resurrection—something that apparently surprised everyone.

When I have to go away (always for work, by the way, and never for fun), my spouse doesn't get that same reaction. It's more like: "Oh that bastard, he's abandoned you and the children for fun and games." Basically, it's as if I had walked out and left everyone to fend for themselves. Then she gets lots of: "You'll be better off without him anyway" and "It's not like he really did anything useful." She gets the sympathy reserved for the deliberately abandoned as opposed to the tragically taken away in their prime that I receive. Anger versus sorrow. It is unclear if either is helpful.

When it comes down to it, the appropriate reaction is: "Oh dear, there goes the division of labor." I'd like to think that that would have been Adam Smith's reaction to these things. The problem is that tasks have to be done, and there is no time for any emotion. It simply means that most tasks take a little more time. Then again, there is time freed up from dealing with each other, so it's not all bad.

Only the tasks and routine activities that really require both of us are an issue. Driving children around to various activities is the main thing. If two things occur at the same time, you're in trouble. If they occur during someone's sleep time, you're in trouble. If they occur too late in the day, you're in trouble. If they occur during school pickup time, you're in trouble. If they require memory (we had a tooth loss that week and a tooth fairy that needed to remember to come), you are most likely in trouble. You just need two or more adults for certain things.

So I missed her very much; I really could have used the extra pair of hands.

PART IV

THE TOUGH

9 Protecting

Occasionally one happens upon a child on a leash. It is usually a harness arrangement decorated with a playful soft-toy motif. My first thought whenever I see this is that the child must be a nightmare. However, more often than not, in direct contrast to the rabid dog image conjured up in my mind, the child is well behaved. The child is also perfectly happy; even more so than dogs usually seem to be. Indeed, the child is happier than most children their age who are forced to walk around with a hand in the air trying to match their parent's pace. That is hardly a model of dignity. By contrast, the leashed child has both hands free and can wander ahead, to the side, or behind before being reigned in. It is not a lot of freedom, but it is much more than the average unleashed child enjoys.

This, however, is beside the point. The main thing about leashes is that the child is far safer in one than in almost any other arrangement you can think of. And the strange thing about our attitude toward leashes is that in almost every other area of child safety, when parents are given the option of doing something that reduces the risk of harm, even slightly, they seem to take it up. Indeed, we often pass laws, without any objection, to make children safe, in case parents don't do it themselves or do not want to voluntarily incur large costs.

So why aren't all children under the age of three required to be on leashes when in public? After all, dogs are.

And there is no controversy when it comes to dogs. First, the dog may be a danger to others. By having the dog under the physical control of a person, that danger is mitigated. Second, the dog may be a danger to itself. It may run away and become lost, it may head toward a construction site, or it may run into traffic. For both of these issues, to a large extent, the older the dog is, the less the danger. But most municipalities require dogs to be leashed regardless of their age.

Now let's come back to human beings under three. All manner of government restrictions are placed on them. For one thing, there is a sharp dividing line in terms of toys. The "not suitable for children under three" label adorns many a promising plaything. For the most part this is because a toy can, when destroyed, have constituent parts that might be a choking hazard. That is, we are concerned that a child may destroy a toy and then attempt, unsuccessfully, to eat it.

So let's build on this. What do you think is more likely to happen to a toddler—that they eat unsuitable toys, or that they escape from a parent and head toward oncoming traffic? In my experience, this comparison is a wash. Much like a dog, they are equally likely to do both. But we don't enforce leashes for children, like we do for dogs. Indeed, there appears to be a taboo against them.

The lack of leashes stands out as an anomaly when it comes to efforts to protect children. For some reason, most of us choose hand holding instead of a leash. But my guess is that if leashes were compulsory, nearly all parents would let go of the hand. In other words, if you had both methods at your disposal, the leash would win. For now, however, it is not even a consideration. Indeed, instead of a leash, parents strap their child into a stroller and push them around. My guess is that had dogs been put in strollers first, rather than on leashes, our norms today would be the other way around.

I raise the discounted protective device of the leash issue as a curiosity, because most of what this chapter is about is exactly the opposite. We engage in continual public debate about things that we need to do to protect children. We seem willing to incur great cost for modest to no gain. To the economist's dispassionate eye, what we put up with is bizarre. But as an economist dad, put up with it I do.

Let's start with an area of continual debate: should we limit the amount of television children watch? Children's television is already highly controlled. Indeed, most jurisdictions legislate to restrict the content that can be broadcast in daylight hours, when we presume that children are awake and vulnerable. But for as long as there has been television, there have been concerns about how much children watch.

For us, access to television is seen as a privilege and not a right. We place a television alluringly in the family room and then place an invisible wall around it saying "off limits." If a request to watch television comes in from one or more household members, it is carefully reviewed by committee;

submissions are taken from all interested parties; the time of the day and the day of the week are considered; and a rigorous check of the applicants' other merits (such as doing homework, asking politely) is done. Then a decision is made, based on guidelines as well as precedent. Unfavorable decisions are usually accompanied by appeals and requirements for the committee to suggest alternative activities (e.g., playing outside or reading a book). Favorable decisions are then referred to a lower-level subcommittee in order to determine what will actually be watched on television.

In an earlier day, without DVDs, that process would have been lengthy enough that a new problem—"there is nothing interesting on TV"—would have come up, and the TV might not actually get turned on. Today, we don't have that luxury, so practices are then reviewed by a nonconsultative panel regarding whether too much TV is being watched overall. In the end, I think a child in our household ends up watching three to five hours of TV per week (yes, per week); about a seventh of the average in the population. For TV-loving parents such as us, this is somewhat surprising (ourselves being in the fifteen-hour-a-week category).

Our household review panel devours any studies that might enlighten us on this issue. The sum total of those studies has been basically uninformative. Some claim TV is plain bad, others claim it depends on what you watch, and others yet say it depends who watches with you. The American Academy of Pediatrics recommends no TV at all for children under two.[1] In the end you need to use your common sense as some of the same outcomes (not getting outdoors, not getting enough exercise) may also apply to things like reading, which I don't hear many people discouraging.

Fortunately for me, economists have gotten into the act. A study by Matthew Gentzkow and Jesse Shapiro[2] uses the fact that television was introduced at different times in different U. S. cities. They have examined the results of standardized tests conducted in the 1960s to look at the long-term effects of television watching. Theoretically, if television is bad, and you had been watching it for twelve years before taking the test—as opposed to four years, or not at all—it would show up in your test performance. Moreover, this was well before the advent of VCRs, so parents had very little ability to choose what their children might watch, and there was certainly no regulation of advertising content.

The study found that there was no negative effect from television watching (at least in terms of high-school test scores). If anything, the effect was positive, and more so for children in non–English-speaking households and where the mother had less than a high-school education.[3]

So can we disband our review process now and just let the kids watch TV until they are sick of it? It would give us more time to watch TV ourselves!

These studies will, of course, do little to stem or resolve the public debate over television—or children's use of any technology that wasn't around in the olden days. But would turning back the clock really protect our children?

As with TV, these days we read time and time again about the dangers of video games. Shoot-'em-up games encourage children to think violent thoughts. Car racing games turn them into reckless drivers. Police games encourage drug trafficking. Space-shooting games foster antialien prejudices. Recently, I bought my eight-year-old daughter *The Dangerous Book for Boys*,[4] to see what some good old-fashioned values might do for her.

Even today, in this iPod generation, that book was an incredible hit. She will not let it leave her sight. It goes everywhere with her and is read all the time. She will happily recite the blurb on the back cover by memory to anyone who asks:

> Recapture Sunday afternoons and long summer days. The perfect book for every boy from eight to eighty.

And what, exactly, makes this book so engrossing? Well, to say it lacks a theme is an understatement. It is just a random set of entries (not even alphabetically ordered) with titles such as "Fossils," "The Laws of Football," "Dinosaurs," "How to Play Poker," "The Origin of Words," and "The Patron Saints of Britain." I mean how many eight-year-olds do you know who aren't fascinated by St. David of Wales and his heroic efforts to establish churches and monasteries in the 500s?

But that's not all. It teaches you about life. For instance, in the entry "Girls" (which takes up a whole page), there is a list of eight points of advice, including the critical message to "be careful about humor," limiting yourself to one joke followed by silence. You just can't buy that kind of information.

So how does it stack up relative to those damned computer games? Pretty well. The entries with the biggest hits were those that compelled activity. Within minutes "the greatest paper airplane ever" whizzed by. But then came pleas for the materials to tackle larger projects. There were calls to make a bow and arrow, a slingshot, a box car, crystals (drugs, I think), a battery (!), tripwires, and finally to go hunting and tan any resulting animal hide. Unlike those computer games, where there is still debate about whether they lead to poor behavior, there is no doubt with this stuff. In this book, there are direct and unequivocal links between the playtime activity and the potentially criminal behavior. After playing computer games, you still need a gun to be violent. But this stuff tells you how to make your own weapon. Things were just clearer in the olden days; and when it comes down to it, kids know when they are just getting virtual stuff as opposed to the real deal. They know when safety is something real that you can grasp in your hands as you extract a poison dart from a younger brother's leg.

Sometimes there is social pressure to take steps that will protect just a few vulnerable children. In 2006, three trees in Milford, Connecticut, were felled to protect a single three-year-old child. The *New York Times* explained why:[5]

> Allergy to nuts is indeed a serious risk to those who have it and requires that parents or caretakers of children always carry a shot of epinephrine to counteract the reaction when there is unintended exposure. On the other hand, the decision is ominous news for trees that reproduce themselves with nuts—walnut, chestnut, pine, pecan, and hazelnut, as well as

> hickory trees. According to the Food Allergy and Anaphylaxis Network, about 0.6 percent, or 1.8 million Americans, are allergic to tree nuts. Making all their neighborhoods safe from nuts could spawn a new logging industry.

The trees were very valuable (arguably more so than a lone child's unsupervised outdoor dalliances—surely a paid supervisor would be cheaper), and so this move spawned considerable controversy. It was seen as child protection gone mad.

The issue here was not whether the town should require the trees to be cut down or not but, instead, who should bear the costs if, indeed, it was worthwhile cutting them down. And there are not just the costs of cutting the trees down but also the loss of their value to surrounding properties. It is not clear whether the risk to the child (or children) is worth the lost trees.

Now if the town had no policy but the risk to the child was truly great, the affected parent, or in this case grandmother, could go to her neighbors and offer compensation for the loss of the trees. If her assessment of the value of that risk wasn't really high enough, then we could conclude that it probably wasn't worth cutting down the trees. However, since the town mandated that the trees be cut down regardless, no such assessment was made, and we will never know what the outcome would have been.

A better policy would be to give the grandmother a right to ask for the trees to be cut down. This would open up the possibility of negotiation again, and the trees might not be cut down if the risks to the child weren't too large. The difference between that and no requirement is simply who bears the costs of cutting down the trees should that be desired—the grandmother or the neighbors. So for issues such as this, the key is to open up the possibility of fruitful negotiation rather than preclude it.

When it comes to school policies prohibiting certain types of food, it may seem that a similar issue arises. Here, we trade off the risk to the child with parental convenience.[6] In this situation, daily negotiations are not possible. The costs would be too high. Instead, a school needs to have a policy on the foods that can be brought in. When the school knows it has a child at risk, something it would have to manage, it sets the policy accordingly. Because children are hard to manage at a young age, it is not surprising that they might think to control the situation by restricting foodstuffs. Schools do this for much food brought in, from meats (which might get bacteria) to sweets (which might cause hyperactivity and create conflicts).

In this situation, the issue might become whether an affected child could go to school at all. And many families may not have the wealth to buy off the convenience costs to other parents. So, in contrast to the trees, there is little possibility of striking an efficient deal here, especially on decisions on the level of whether to allow kids to bring in cookies or not.

In my mind, the way to think about schools is very simple: social risk pooling. Someone's child may have a nut allergy. Yours may have something else. For instance, they might be poorly behaved, requiring the deployment of extra teaching resources. In each case, managing the issue may cause inconvenience or cost to others. But ask yourself, "If that were my child, would I expect the school to accommodate him or her?"

If the answer is yes, then you should support whatever arrangements the school makes.

While only some children need protection because of allergies, a wide range of government policies—happily supported by voters—are designed to protect children from potential parental neglect of their safety. I already mentioned safety standards for toys. As a result of the labeling, first-time parents fret about what they purchase for their children until they're three and then buy whatever they want after that—even though there may be another vulnerable sibling wandering around the house. What should they do? Keep the older children restricted to under-three toys forever? The solution is unclear, but at the very least, the standard raises awareness.

But what of that other bane of a parent's life: car seats? When I was growing up, there were no such things. We were dropped in the back seat with a simple lap belt (if that), never to experience the comfort of a full-restraint seat as children do today. Of course, we were too short to see anything but sky out the window, but no one really seemed to care.

Sometime during the ensuing decades, scientists put child-size crash test dummies in cars and found out that they did not fare too well in crashes. The end result was an evolving car seat that cocooned babies and then older children in a protective layer. During the same period, over-the-shoulder belts became standard in cars, but, for the most part, a generation has leap-frogged over that option.

Before we consider the myriad of potential benefits here, as an economist I would be remiss in not discussing the price of technology. First of all, there is the car seat itself, which can cost hundreds of dollars. Then there is the installation, which needs to be done properly and can be time consuming. These days anchors are required, so it is not simply a matter of plugging your child's seat into a seat-belt socket. It is a twenty-minute job. So following on from that is the inevitable second car seat if you have two cars, rather than moving one around. You've doubled your costs right there.

Next, add the costs of strapping a child in—or worse still, multiple children. This is not a pretty exercise, especially in winter when they may or may not be wearing a coat, thus requiring you to adjust the straps. These are issues you just don't face with a lap-and-shoulder seat belt. And as the family grows, so does the space devoted to car seats. I have wondered if the trend to larger cars or SUVs is actually driven by the requirements to have car seats and the fact that children aren't allowed to sit in the front seats. If you have three car seats and one child has a friend over, you suddenly need a seven-seat car. And that's just to give you the option of being able to manage normal social logistics. Now we're talking about thousands of extra dollars.

And, finally, there's the whole issue of what to do when you don't have a car seat. If you take it all seriously, you'll need to avoid buses, trains, and taxis. But what if you travel? Do you take a car seat and install it in your rented car? Will it be damaged in flight?

The costs are considerable. So each time my family incurs some of those costs, I have to remind myself of the benefit; I am saving a life here. Apparently, I am willing to go to great lengths to do that.

Sadly, it appears that my rationale for logistical sacrifice may not be too strong. Certainly, the crash test dummies fare better in car seats, but what happens with live children and imperfect parents? Steve Levitt, of Freakonomics fame, has taken a look at the wealth of actual crash statistics.[7] Taking into account lots of other factors—such as what caused a car crash, who else was in the car, what the weather was like, and so forth—he was able to compare the performance of car seats with both lap and lap-and-shoulder belts. His conclusion: car seats prevent fatalities and injuries for those under two, but if you take an older child (between two and six) out of their car seat and just use a lap-and-shoulder belt, there isn't much improvement in their chances of avoiding death or serious injury. In some car crashes, such as rear-enders, car seats actually perform worse.

When I proudly brought this excellent piece of econometric research home to show that we could free up some space in the car, I was quickly informed that our household behavior would not be changing. We would have car seats all around until they were well beyond six years old. Well, we had the seats anyway (five or six at my last count, between various cars and ages, and a total expenditure of $1,000).

Herein lies the stickiness of the safety situation. It is tough to go back when you don't have to, even when the cost is high. And there is some logic to it all. Even Levitt found that child safety seats maximized the chances of a "no child injury" crash; although only by 1.6 percentage points. But all of these improvements pale in comparison to improved driving, avoiding heavy-traffic routes, driving shorter distances, and so forth. The safety seat appears to be far from the defining factor in safety.

Levitt's results will be probed and prodded before anyone, especially governments, seriously considers changing behavior and standards. And appropriately so. But consider the difficulty of changing back, even if the evidence was uncontroversial. A government would have to decide that the costs were not worth the mandate and then face electoral punishment every time a child wearing a seat belt was injured. The risk aversion of parents filters up into the political sphere.

Interestingly, it appears from Levitt's research that parents are willing to pay with their lives, or at least the lives of passenger adults, to get small improvements in safety for their children. He found that if you had to choose between an adult and a child being in the front seat of a car when there was a crash, you could significantly minimize the likelihood that someone would die by putting the adult in the back. Every weekend, we make the opposite choice. Moreover, even when there is a free seat in the back, we leave the adults up front. As with the child leashes, this suggests some sort of taboo.

Of course, putting an adult in the back seat with a baby might be beneficial. And a New Zealand study has shown that babies might actually stop breathing while asleep in car seats.[8] While the Levitt study has been controversial, the New Zealand study is not. And the solution is apparently to have one parent sit in the back and monitor the situation. I am pretty sure this will zap the remaining fun out of driving somewhere and confine us all to home until the baby safely grows up.

There is, of course, good news in all this for commercial entrepreneurs in child safety. Parents are willing to pay considerable amounts for small improvements—perceived or real—in child safety. In the case of baby seats, I'm sure some head adjustment to prevent the breathing problem will be available soon. But one wonders how far the whole exercise might go. Suppose I developed a cocoon-type restraint whereby you took your children, put them in a coffinlike structure with a little window to look out of and staked them neatly in the trunk of the car or SUV. I'm pretty sure I could get some engineer to demonstrate the safety benefits of this. Couple this with the alluring idea of having the kids out of sight while driving (whine free!), and I think it is a winning product idea.

Parental craving for child safety (subject to wealth constraints) seems practically unlimited, and the best example of inelastic demand that we are ever going to find. We are yet to see the "safe and silent cocoon," of course. Maybe that is because of its leashlike qualities. But if it were to become available, I may well be first in line. Rather than the children, perhaps it is I who could use some restraint.

10 Punishing

There is an incident that I remember as if it were yesterday. Child No. 1 must have been about two then, and it was dinner-time. For some weeks she had been digging her heels in and refusing to eat what was put in front of her. Instead, she would fall back on the staples of fruit and yogurt. We were sick of the nightly struggle.

This time, we decided to try something completely different. We warned her that if she threw a tantrum about dinner, she would be put straight to bed. No dinner, no bath, no story. You can guess what happened next. She threw a tantrum and to her horror found herself in bed minutes later. It was 5:30 p.m., and there was no way she was going to sleep soon. But it was done.

The whole issue was a dilemma. What if this didn't work? What if she threw another tantrum tomorrow at breakfast? How long could we hold out? Were we going down a path we would never be able to recover from? Restricting food was against every instinct we had up until that point. We had to remind ourselves of the obvious: she would not starve. She would eat again—and, given her love of food, probably quite soon.

She calmed down but was clearly not going to be able to sleep for a while. Given that the main punishment was "not having dinner," we decided to let her get up for a while, until her actual bedtime. But we did not relent on dinner.

She had been up for just a short while when she came to me and asked the question that made this experience truly unforgettable. "Daddy," she said with beseeching eyes, "are you going to give me food tomorrow?"

This exposed a flaw in our punishment. She had no conception that this was just a one-time situation. In her mind, it was entirely possible that the whole eating thing was over. I would be amazed if a straighter arrow to a parent's heart existed beyond that question at that moment.

It felled me. But being the tough game theorist I was, I didn't immediately offer her some ice cream. I stuck with the program. "Yes, you can eat tomorrow. Missing dinner was just for tonight. So long as you don't throw a tantrum, you can have breakfast tomorrow."

"OK," she nodded. And that is what happened. No tantrum and a big breakfast. And what was more, the punishment had a lasting effect—there were no more tantrums, at least on that subject.

This story encapsulates everything that is tough about punishing children. What behavior triggers a punishment? What punishment should you use? How do you explain the rules to your children? Will it work? And how do you deal with the fact that punishment is costly to the punisher as well as the punished, perhaps more so?

The punishment of children periodically surfaces as a public debate about whether spanking should be outlawed. There are two underlying issues here. The first is the fact that violence—even restrained beating—is outlawed between adults. The second is whether spanking children might damage them in some way. The former is enough to convince me not to spank our children, but the idea of outlawing it for everyone has to be based, in the first instance, on the evidence. If it turned out that the evidence was favorable (that is, it did little harm and helped with discipline), then we would have to move on to morals to deal with the policy issue.

But it appears that the evidence, while mixed, ultimately stacks up against spanking. As reported in *Slate*:[1]

> One study stands out: An effort by University of California at Berkeley psychologist Diana Baumrind to tease out the effects of occasional spanking compared to frequent spanking and no spanking at all. Baumrind tracked about one-hundred white, middle-class families in the East Bay area of northern California from 1968 to 1980. The children who were hit frequently were more likely to be maladjusted. The ones who were occasionally spanked had slightly higher misbehavior scores than those who were not spanked at all. But this difference largely disappeared when Baumrind accounted for the children's poor behavior at a younger age. In other words, the kids who acted

out as toddlers and preschoolers were more likely to act out later, whether they were spanked occasionally or never. Lots of spanking was bad for kids. A little didn't seem to matter.

This seems broadly sensible and likely. Repeated spanking as a punishment is problematic. It could suggest that parents are unrestrained and rely on it too readily. Alternatively, it could suggest that for some children it simply does not work as a punishment. To just keep doing it over and over doesn't help.

Economics has lots to say on issues like this. The economic theory of punishment is simple—a punishment is like a price: set it at a high enough level to deter behavior. If the offender understands this, the possibility of punishment will deter the behavior, and no punishment will actually be given. When punishments work to deter behavior, they do not need to be repeated.

So if spanking is used as a punishment repeatedly, that probably means it isn't working. Add to that the evidence that repeating this type of punishment causes damage, and you have a real case for a policy outlawing repeated spanking. That would probably involve outlawing the whole lot and just prosecuting the worst offenders.

Notions that spanking is "the only thing a child will understand" would not affect the policy here. Repeated spanking indicates that the child does not understand it after all, and if that leaves a parent with nothing in the toolkit, so be it. The point here is that spanking should not really be in the toolkit in the first place. The other point, as I heard somewhere, is that this same argument extends to absurdity. For instance, it also applies to foreign tourists who need directions; a mild flogging is the only thing they will understand!

But the same principle—repetition means failure—applies to any sort of punishment. When it comes down to it, even those like me who refuse to engage in any physical pain as punishment could still be doing their kids harm. Shouting, incarceration, and other forms of punishment are not guaranteed to be any less emotionally damaging. And their repetition will likely generate the same ill effects as spanking.

We worry often that shouting all the time at the kids might do them damage. Sometimes a good verbal shellacking just comes from the gut, and let's face it, it's more likely to occur when we are tired, hungry, or stressed. Other times, you need to find a muse to convey appropriate disdain for the offense committed. My inspiration comes from James Earl Jones as Darth Vader—I lower my voice an octave or two and use the child's full name, including their middle name. This certainly generates fear, but use it too often and it loses effectiveness.

People rely on shouting because it is easy. But that is precisely the feature that makes it a poor candidate for behavioral improvement. The problem, as the opening story in this chapter showed, is that the best punishments are costly to the parent as well as the child, which is why we can be reluctant to enact them, even after some behavioral offense has been committed. But once you show that reluctance, the threat of a punishment just isn't *credible*.

This is something Nobel Laureate Thomas Schelling realized early in his career. He spent much of his time worrying about how the United States and the Soviet Union could avoid turning the Cold War into a real war. He observed that the issues in negotiating with the Russians were very similar to the issues in negotiating with one's child. If the Russians decided to escalate hostilities, one side might be tempted to use nuclear weapons. However, that could ultimately prove too costly to really carry out. And faced with that, the Russians might tempt fate. Similarly, a child can understand whether a threat is really credible or not and adjust their behavior accordingly.

What this means is that, if we're going to use punishment at all, we need to find strategies that we are actually willing to carry out at the appropriate time. Getting fed up with repeated behavior can motivate this, but in reality the best punishment is one with such a threat value that it never needs to be carried out. And for that, you need to choose your weapon carefully. The ideal would be to get to a situation where you can say to a child contemplating an offense, "Are you feeling lucky, punk? Go ahead, make my day," just like Clint Eastwood did in *Sudden Impact* to such good effect.

In our house, one of the main forms of real punishment is the dreaded "corner"—that is, incarceration. Our house doesn't actually have many corners—some rabid architect did away with them—but the place called "the corner" is a little, dark space just inside the door to the garage. Being sent to the corner means isolation, but also a mild chance of being hit by an

Tulsa City-County Library
Central Library

Checked Out Items 4/2/2017 13:34
XXXXXXXXXX0221

Item Title	Due Date
President Pennybaker / Kate Feiffer ; illustrated by Diane Goode.	4/17/2017
The magic mustache / by Gary Barwin ; illustrated by Stephane Jorisch.	4/17/2017
You and me : we're opposites / by Harriet Ziefert ; illustrated by Ethan Long.	4/17/2017
Found / Salina Yoon.	4/17/2017
Giraffes can't dance [sound recording] / book by Giles Andreae [illustrated by] Guy Parker-Rees.	4/17/2017
What is part this, part that? / Harriet Ziefert ; illustrations by Tom Slaughter.	4/17/2017

To renew:
www.tulsalibrary.org
918-549-7444

We value your feedback.
Please take our online survey
www.tulsalibrary.org/Z45

in-swinging door (so I guess there is a possibility of physical punishment in our household!).

Many offenses can lead to the corner: rudeness, tantrums, violence toward siblings, inability to resolve arguments, or refusal to obey "orders." So the punishment is dealt out quite frequently. But it is not often repeated for the same offense.

We also have higher levels of punishment. Corner first, then denial of television, sent to room, and sent to bed early can all be employed. Occasionally, things get out of hand. One day Child No. 1, aged three, refused to do pretty much anything. The situation escalated until she was in her room, hungry and screaming, with no toys. Not a pretty moment, nor a proud one for me, and it required a second parent to resolve the whole thing. But that is the exception that proved the rule. In that situation, none of the punishments worked. Something else was going on that needed more effort to resolve.

Our second eldest was another matter. Whereas our daughter would be dutifully distressed at being sent to the corner (something that indicated to me that the message had been delivered), our son wouldn't react that way at all. He would happily go to the corner. Sometimes we would hear him singing: "I'm in the corner, I'm in the corner." It was a merry ditty, and it often triggered discussions as to whether it was working. But it must have been, because the behavior was never repeated. That is the real measure of success.

A part of me enjoys being more innovative about punishments than simple cornering. This is a good way of lowering the costs; make the children believe you enjoy it. In particular, I like irony. Failure to share a toy properly can lead to confiscation. Confiscation does not mean the toy is removed from sight.

Instead, it is put on a high shelf—on display for all to see and not forget. Of course, real irony would be to take the toy and slice it in half. I have threatened this but have not yet had to carry it out.

Yes, irony can be very effective. Child No. 1 once took a chocolate without permission. As she came out of her room, she seemed to be chewing on something. Ever suspicious, I interrogated her: "Where is the wrapper?" For some reason, still quite young at the time, she was shocked I had worked out her deception. So she dutifully got the wrapper from its hiding place under her bed. That time I didn't have to punish her. Irony did the work for me. I said that if she ever did that again (technically, if she was caught doing it again), we would remove every special treat from the house. She was old enough to understand that her currently low chance of having a treat would fall to zero if we didn't actually have any around. Years later she still remembers this potential punishment and has taught it to her younger siblings.

But you don't always have the time or energy to be creative. It is there that credibility can come in handy. If you have a solid reputation, as I do now, magic can happen. I often abandon the hard work of selecting a punishment altogether. So when I am not getting compliance with a request or order—such as getting ready for bath or bed—I simply stand there and close my eyes. You see, I know that the children's imaginations are much more active than my own. "I am thinking up a suitable punishment," I say, "and if, when I open my eyes, you haven't done X, I will tell you what it is." A flurry of activity always ensues. I don't think I've *ever* had to actually think up a punishment—and who knows what they think it might be, if I ever did! Technically, in this situation there is no punishment, just a credible threat of punishment. It will be interesting to see if this ever comes up in a future therapy session.

Of course, the threat of punishment is the ideal. The hard part is building up a reputation for tough action. Game theory teaches us that working in small steps can help here. For example, Child No. 2 had a habit of not flushing the toilet, and I had a habit of discovering it some hours later. I guess one could contemplate ironic punishments here, but none are really appropriate.

The problem was that the offense was usually discovered too late, and what is more, it was really only occurring once a day—so there was not much opportunity for intensive learning. He needed to be aware of it at the time so he could form a flushing habit. Monitoring the situation was one option, but who has the time for that? So instead I punished him by denying access to his favorite Web site (*Club Penguin*, I think it was) for a day. But that wasn't all.

I outlined a path of ever-increasing punishments on the same theme. If I discovered tomorrow that he had done (or not done) it again, then he would lose *Club Penguin* for a week. And then if, on the day after, he did it again, he would lose *Club Penguin* for a month. And after that, he would lose it forever. Of course, this last one would be sufficient to do the job, but a random act of forgetfulness could put us in a war scenario, and perhaps one where the punishment exceeded the crime.

Now the next day he did forget, and the week-long ban was on. But he was really worried after that. A couple more indiscretions, and it might be the end of the game forever. That fear was enough to jog his mind whenever he went to do his business. Since then, the habit has formed, and we get along just fine.

This scheme works because, first, it is not too costly to carry out initially, and, second, with each punishment the child loses in two ways: they incur the initial penalty and also have an increased risk of a worse fate. The combination works as if you had imposed the worst possible punishment. Talk about having your cake and eating it too.

One problem with trying to be credible is that you can make mistakes. The common one is punishing a child and then finding out they didn't do it. When the children were young, I would just shrug my shoulders, say "oops," and elect not to tell them. I know this isn't fair, but there is a bigger picture here, and it doesn't happen that often. After all, think of all the things they should be punished for but we don't know about. Next time they might actually commit the offense. All in all, it is best to hush it up. The system balances out on average.

But when they get older and they realize this type of thing, legitimate protests occur. Recently, when Child No. 2 came back from swimming, his mother could not find his bathing suit in his bag. Not only that, his spare suit was missing too. It was not the first time this had happened, but previously it had been realized before everyone arrived home, and the bathing suit was duly rescued.

Forgetfulness is not something we want to encourage, so he received a punishment. On Friday nights the family sits down to watch *Survivor*. That week he missed out. He was upset and kept on claiming that he "didn't know" how this could have happened (for good reason, as it turned out). Those protests of innocence fell on deaf ears.

The next day, his mother found the bathing suits—both of them—in his bag exactly where they should have been. Oops. Indeed, this was the second such incident in as many weeks. The previous week, he had been accused of misplacing his school pants at home, something that seemed to me a hard thing to do. Turns out someone had mistakenly put his pants away in his sister's closet. Double oops.

Each time, the accuser was his mother. The evidence was irrefutable. What could we do? First up, we made amends for the unfair punishment. I offered him a "free pass": the next time he did something that was due a punishment, he would get off with just a warning. As that was likely to be in the near future, he was happy with the deal.

But we also had to consider the false accusation, which (a) had not been a one-time occurence and, most important, (b) did not involve me. I suggested that he be allowed to think up a punishment for her. That created amusement all around—well, except for one person. But it was accepted.

He struggled with what type of punishment to dole out. He toyed with sending her to bed early but quickly realized that wasn't a punishment at all; and if he hadn't realized it, I would have pointed it out. Then he naturally gravitated toward the "eye for an eye" philosophy. "Next time on *Survivor*, you won't be watching, Mommy."

He started to speculate on whether that was enough or whether she should also be forced to sit through *The Wiggles* while we all watched her. I loved his sense of irony but pointed out that the extra bit was really just for his amusement and that perhaps he didn't want us to start adding things we found amusing to punishments too. So he left it at reciprocity.

This was a satisfying outcome, and no doubt his mother will think twice before accusing him of crimes in the future. Of course, I suspect it is only a matter of time before his older sister, who is very risk averse, hits on the idea of prepunishment: you know, can you punish me now so that if the next one falls at a time that might be inconvenient or uncertain, she has one in the bank. It is an interesting idea, but I suspect there's a reason one cannot pay for parking tickets in advance. You want the punishment cost to be immediate and linked to the activity.

As it turned out, my son's next crime was committed in the ordinary course of events. He wasn't the only one who was happy. Conveniently, it saved both of us from the costs of punishment.

11 Sharing

It is readily apparent to most children that the fundamental economic problem—that is, that there isn't enough to go around—is relevant to their lives at almost every turn. The clear manifestation of this comes as soon as another child enters into their realm without their own stock of toys. Both children know that someone is going to miss out on playing with a particular toy, and, by golly, it isn't going to be them.

The first reaction of a child to all of this is a defensive one: claim ownership over all and sundry, usually accompanied by one of their earliest spoken words, "mine." (And not to put too fine a point on it, they understand this concept well before they understand how to tell red from blue, men from women, and wees from poos.) In some instances, this leads to a physical fight that parents have to break up and then try to broker some sort of agreement. This usually involves diplomatic language: an acknowledgment of long-term ownership but a respect for the value of having visitors. To be sure, that carefully articulated language is not for the benefit of the children—whose understanding of "long-term" and "respect" is tenuous at best—but to exhibit to the other parent that you understand the broader philosophical issues at hand.

That is just the start. The next phase in social development involves an education as to the appropriate norm of fairness with regard to toy scarcity—namely, the idea of taking turns. This involves considerable parental stress as your child receives a toy that you will then ask them to part with at some near point in the future. Their failure to do so without fuss is a blight on you as the parent. Once again, embarrassment is the source of stress rather than your fear of not being able to physically wrest the toy from your child if need be.

But if all goes well, it is possible to reach parental nirvana. A child comes into your house, and your child, without prompting, offers that child a turn with a toy. There is no higher feeling of parental satisfaction and smugness than this, not to mention the fact that it gives you (and I guess your child) the moral high ground should their counterpart not play ball. Sadly, all of this effort between the ages of two and four is not really enough to stop your child developing into an adult who will backstab others at work to climb the corporate ladder; but then, that isn't really the point.

Our eldest daughter cottoned on to the principle of fairness very early in life. Indeed, her defining catchphrase, to this day, is "That's not fair." However, while she understands the broad principle—that is, we want things to be fair so no one loses out—her implementation is somewhat different: no one should get more than her. In mathematical terms, she isn't into equality (=) so much as inequality (<).

Claims of unfairness can get quite tiresome. "He got to go to a birthday party today and I didn't." "He got less vegetables than me." "She already had a turn." On the face of it, each of these seems like a sound argument. However, given that there are no similar cries of unfairness when she gets more, in the broader scheme of things, it can get downright annoying. Moreover, sometimes her argument often implies that the benefit bestowed on her siblings should be taken away to restore justice. The idea that things might be taken away for no actual gain to another really offends my economic sensibilities.

Anyhow, the best place to turn to deal with annoying legalistic behavior is, of course, legal philosophy. In my case, I turned to John Rawl's *Theory of Justice*. The Rawlsian idea is that we should think about justice from the perspective that "you could have been born them." Since we're mostly risk averse, this means that justice should try and make things work out so that you wouldn't care whether you were born yourself or someone else.

So I apply the same logic to my daughter. Every time she claims that some little thing is unfair in relation to a younger sibling, I offer her a deal. "OK, you can have that but you have to have everything else they have too." And if I am feeling particularly devious, I add, "And they will get what you have. You can swap lives."

That pretty much puts an end to it. Faced with that choice, it turns out she is happy with her lot in life relative to her siblings. She certainly wouldn't want them to get what she has. Justice is served every time.

All this progress in judicial philosophy took an interesting turn when Child No. 1 (at the age of eight) discovered the notion of a contract. She was complaining that her mother kept reneging on promises. She would promise one thing and then, when the time came to deliver, she would change it or move it further into the future. This was, of course, all true.

So we had a discussion as to what to do about it. I suggested that perhaps she would like to get things in writing the next time Mommy made a promise.

"What good would that do?'

"Well you would have a record of what the promise is."

"So what? She'll just change it again."

"In that case you could point out that it is a binding contract."

"What does 'binding contract' mean?"

"It means that if Mommy doesn't keep her promise, the government will step in to enforce it."

"Really, how?"

"You could take Mommy to court, and a judge would order her to keep her promise."

With that she whipped open Microsoft Word and drew herself up a contract, including her consideration: not to complain unless the promise was broken. Her mother was surprised to get the contract, in duplicate, but signed it anyhow.

The next day, I found myself being presented with my own contract. I had, over dinner, promised to let my daughter stay up late over the spring break if she went to bed early leading up to it. An hour later I was asked to sit down and sign a contract to that effect, including the, now standard, "no complaint" clause. I happily signed, our signatures were witnessed, and the contract was filed away.

I was a little worried that I had opened a can of worms here. Everything had suddenly gone from informal to highly legalistic. I guess our daughter had a few trust issues. But in reality, I have no complaints. It is, after all, the adult way of dealing with things.

Getting children to behave like "good adults" is, of course, the big picture here. The little steps toward cooperation that we try to implement when they are toddlers are relatively easy compared with the social values we try to instill in them in adolescence. Let's face it, if world leaders reacted as well as toddlers to moves toward sharing and cooperation, we would quickly have world peace.

The struggle here is exemplified by a Seattle school that banned Legos. Well, they didn't so much ban Legos as put them aside for awhile while property rights rules could be established. Thankfully, the teachers published an account of how they arrived at their decision, so we can take a look at what might have been going on.[1]

As toys go, Lego is pretty good on the sharing front. There are usually plenty of pieces, allowing more than one child to play. However, at that school, conversations like this were commonplace.

"I'm making an airport and landing strip for my guy's house. He has his own airplane," said Oliver.

"That's not fair!" said Carl. "That takes too many cool pieces and leaves not enough for me."

"Well, I can let other people use the landing strip, if they have airplanes," said Oliver. "Then it's fair for me to use more cool pieces, because it's for public use."

To my economic mind, this is actually quite heartening. I love the public good argument—you know, my use has higher benefits for more people—and for a time, it generated a good outcome.

> Discussions like the one above led to children collaborating on a massive series of Lego structures we named Legotown. Children dug through hefty-sized bins of Legos, sought "cool pieces," and bartered and exchanged until they established a collection of homes, shops, public facilities, and community meeting places. We carefully protected Legotown from errant balls and jump ropes, and watched it grow day by day.
>
> Sadly, the cooperative spirit didn't last.
>
> A group of about eight children conceived and launched Legotown. Other children were eager to join the project, but as the city grew—and space and raw materials became more precious—the builders began excluding other children. Occasionally, Legotown leaders explicitly rebuffed children, telling them that they couldn't play. Typically the exclusion

was more subtle, growing from a climate in which Legotown was seen as the turf of particular kids. The other children didn't complain much about this; when asked about Legos, they'd often comment vaguely that they just weren't interested in playing with Legos anymore. As they closed doors to other children, the Legotown builders turned their attention to complex negotiations among themselves about what sorts of structures to build, whether these ought to be primarily privately owned or collectively used, and how "cool pieces" would be distributed and protected. These negotiations gave rise to heated conflict and to insightful conversation.

But even this state of affairs did not last long. Legotown was accidentally destroyed (yes, an actual accident), and the older children refused to relinquish their ownership of the pieces. The teachers intervened and banned Legos. They were worried about the power relationships and thought the children needed some education on authority, ownership, and inequality.

Now the kids here were aged between five and nine. The teachers were concerned that the older ones didn't appreciate the power they had over the others and the apparently arbitrary nature of all this. They turned the Lego experience into a trading game so that everyone got some Legos. However, that was stacked against the older kids, which, and this shouldn't be a shock, they didn't like one bit. It turns out they objected to being arbitrarily put at the bottom of society. Funnily enough, so do grown-ups.

I wasn't there to appreciate the whole situation, so it is probably not appropriate to be judgmental—but were the teachers out of their friggin' minds? Let's be very clear about this. A group of eight older children undertook an activity that involved the creation of an entire town out of Legos, taking them two months to build. They were protective of it and excluded younger children who, quite plausibly, might have spent much of their time destroying the older kids' vision. You only have to observe this behavior first-hand to see it arise time and time again. It is an issue of control.

So quite understandably, when faced with the destruction they had tried so long to prevent, the older children's immediate reaction was to maintain control. They didn't see it as an opportunity to spread the wealth in a brave new world. They were mourning their lost creation and were not ready to move on. As a result of this, they lost everything, and then were subjected to "lessons" in power and authority as the losers in society.

What disturbs me is that this was, as these things go, a very positive activity. There were eight kids who had formed a group to build Legotown. They had taken pride in it and had learned to work together and protect themselves from outside interference. Most of the time, one kid takes over and all is lost quickly. This activity sustained itself and was well above average for collective behavior. The fact that it involved age segregation is just too bad. You can't have everything.

The teachers didn't see it that way and acted in a way that seems to punish the older children. The older kids' explanations about what was going on are no less sophisticated than most adults' would be. They hadn't devolved into *Lord of the Flies* or anything like it.

As I see it, the issue was not about Legotown; beyond question, for me, the children who built the town, owned the town. The issue here was about the Lego pieces themselves. That was the scarce resource. If the older children were monopolizing them, that was the problem. The appropriate response would surely have been to ration the Legos and distribute them more fairly. If the older children wanted more Legos, they would have to do deals with others. The idea that the thing they owned was gone if it was destroyed is surely too much. Do we have to give up our land if our house burns down? Was that the message?

But don't get me wrong, the teachers were entirely well meaning. They show a clear concern in their account about how best to teach children about fairness and society. It isn't easy to do this. What worries me is not their views about that—in my experience, many teachers share them—it is that they might have chosen the wrong moment, thus rendering their lesson ineffective (and potentially harmful). I also think the children probably did understand the forces at work. They understood inequality based on age—which they themselves suffered from in other situations. Contrast that with the later trading game, which based inequality on something more arbitrary; it was clearly stacked against them.

This example tells us much about how children view and respond to ownership. In my experience, different individuals respond in different ways. Let me return to my own experience. My eldest child sees ownership as an "option value." She likes to own things just in case she needs them later on. So she will hoard and acquire anything. Nothing is immune from this, and her room is a monument to it. As an economist, I find the sheer waste of resources distressing, but that's just how she is.

Child No. 2, on the other hand, sees ownership as the ability to deny others access. He couldn't really care less about owning stuff and never tries to wrest ownership from others. But if you give him something of his own, he loves it. He uses the toy or whatever and takes good care of it. This is exactly what we want ownership to mean.

The two extremes here represent what is right and wrong about ownership; but perhaps not in the way you think. My son's view emphasizes the caring and use role of ownership—it encourages things to be used efficiently and appropriately. My daughter's view emphasizes the accumulation and creating role of ownership—it encourages things to be made and acquired in the first place. Society requires both to function efficiently. Having just one leads to inefficiency—through either waste or forgone opportunity.

The kids in Seattle employed both. They owned enough material to create, and they excluded enough others to maintain what they were doing. If only more adults could work out that compromise as effectively.

The sharing I've been talking about thus far in this chapter has been fairly personal. But we also encourage our kids to think more broadly in sharing—say, through charitable giving. The problem here is that the recipient tends to be anonymous, making it hard for the children to relate to their trials enough to actually part with something.

To take an example, like many households with school-age kids, our family spends one month a year motivated to read ever greater quantities of books under the guise of the MS Readathon. This is an annual fundraising exercise for research into multiple sclerosis. The idea is that your child finds sponsors, each of whom agrees to donate an amount for every book they read. The assumption is that parents (also donating an amount per book) will monitor the reading and ensure it is all on the up and up. All in all, it is a win–win situation: children are encouraged to read, and a good cause raises money. Our two older kids managed thirty-five books between them, enough to qualify for a prize.

The MS Readathon has been going on for at least three decades across many countries. A friend of mine in the United States, now a successful lawyer, participated a quarter of a century ago but with very different motivations. Her reading shattered all records for quantity. She won a school prize and the adulation of all. But that isn't what motivated her.

The slogan for the MS Readathon was, and still is, "Read for a cure." Well, my friend took that literally. She surmised that sometime in the past, someone had discovered the cure for MS. However, due to bureaucratic incompetence or fate or something, the precise book that contained the cure was lost. So the idea was to read as many books as possible in search for the cure!

But generally, the MS Readathon bumbles along in much the same way as raffles or fundraising chocolates do. Even when children dye their hair or cut it for cancer research (a nice sense of radicalism), there is no pure giving. Many children still see only what the donors are getting and not that they are giving.

As for my friend, she never found the cure for MS, but she was a greater contributor to the cause as a result. Who knows how she would have done with "shave for a cure"?

PART V

THE FUN

12 Playing

To an economist, playing should mean just that: playing. It should be something of pure leisure. No work, only satisfaction.

But often child's play doesn't fit into that category. Our children are expected to "play nice," and so we tag little lessons in social values onto their interactions with other children. Our children are expected to "play fair" and basically keep to the rules rather than, say, win. And we ration the activities that we regard as appropriate play. These days we tend to favor imaginative play over passive activities and board games over video games. All these activities involve some sort of work tagged on the back of play.

Personally, I enjoy passive activities such as watching television, and I think that a good video game can often be superior to a routine board game. I want my children to play to win; and playing nice isn't always that much fun. So why should I expect these other things of my children? Suffice it to say, and this is no real surprise, my own feelings and the expectations of other adults don't mix too well on the subject of play.

It is, of course, interesting to watch children play with one another. A while ago, I observed my eldest (then seven) and her brother (then five) playing chess. They had the actual rules down, but this typically leads to a quick bloodbath by the strategic (seven) over the aesthetic (five). Strategic play, thinking about how your opponent will react to your moves, is the intended mode of chess. Aesthetic play is something quite different. Here you are moving pieces to increase the likelihood that they will make interesting patterns. A good example of strategic play is the two-knight opening move—and this has the added benefit of being aesthetically pleasing as well.

Following the first game, they decided to change the rules. Mr. Aesthetic decided on a new layout for the two rows of starting pieces, and Ms. Strategic saw an opportunity and decided that a flexible starting layout was a good idea. So a new set of rules was agreed upon. All the pieces would move according to the same rules but would start differently.

Ms. Strategic continued a defensive posture with pawns in the front row, while Mr. Aesthetic offered up a mixture led by two rooks in the center, while the king and queen sat at each end of the back row, surrounded by a set of pawns. The new rules lasted two moves (actually, one) before Mr. Aesthetic swept across the board to remove a pawn. That move was "reversed" when a new rule came up—the "no-taking period." (Yes, it was called that.) This was a period of indeterminate time (well, to the observer, but not to Ms. Strategic, who would announce when it was over) whereby they could move pieces but were not allowed to take anyone else's. This resulted in lots of repositioning until Ms. Strategic got frustrated that Mr. Aesthetic wouldn't muck up his beautiful king-queen-pawn configurations to allow her instant victory when the "no-taking period" finally ended.

The game took some time, because Ms. Strategic had to wipe out all of Mr. Aesthetic's pieces before he would budge on protecting the King. It occurred to me that this form of play was far closer to real warfare than the actual rules of chess. The continued negotiation of the rules through a diplomatic process that required everyone to still want to fight, along with the strategic manipulation of that process, led to a situation far closer to historical experience.

Anyhow, the new rules lasted only one game; Mr. Aesthetic soon decided that it would look better if he could use both black *and* white pieces in his two rows. Ms. Strategic was very upset by this notion, claiming it would lead to chaos because no one would know whose pieces where theirs. A good point, but Mr. Aesthetic countered that the King and Queen would be a common color, and that would define the game. Negotiations broke down at that point, and Professor Diplomat (me) was brought in to broker a solution.

I suggested that they use pieces from an additional, different-looking chess set, thereby satisfying both Mr. Aesthetic's desires and Ms. Strategic's concerns. Alas, they took this to mean that both sets of chess pieces plus a set of checkers could be used on a single board. It took them some time to get past the "laying-out period," but they finally worked out that no one could actually move—thus handing Mr. Aesthetic a victory of sorts.

Eventually a hybrid game evolved where the chess pieces were laid out in the normal configuration while the checker pieces filled the remaining rows. (The other chess set was used for a second game, played simultaneously.) First, there was a game of checkers in the constrained space until one player lost all their checker pieces; then they could use chess pieces to take the other's checker pieces. However, the hybrid involved no change in rules, as I observed when a checker piece leapt over a knight to take it! The chess pieces appear to be at a considerable disadvantage. The goal, however, remains to get the chess king.

This game of meta-chess is far more interesting than chess itself; especially as a spectator sport.

It is, of course, important to play games with your children rather than just watching them play. But let's face it, joining in is often really boring. So I compensate by having some fun myself, at the risk of hurting their feelings.

My attitude toward playing games with children is simple: I play to win. I see no need to coddle my children in game playing. If they want that, they can go elsewhere, say, to their mother. How my children play games with each other is very personality driven; how they play with me is another matter.

At the age of three, children form the cognitive ability to play games. They understand the rules and seem to understand the difference between winning and losing. The first game for us was “Snap!” In this card game, you pick up cards and put them down until two match; then you compete by quickly saying “snap” and slapping your hand down to claim the lot. The game continues until one player holds all the cards.

My daughter (Ms. Strategic from the previous story) learned this game from her mother. It was a rather relaxed affair. Then she turned her attention to me. I snapped the snappiest snap one could imagine. The game was over pretty quickly, and she didn’t get a look in. Not surprisingly, she claimed it was all unfair and that she needed a turn. I took a hard line, and the snap session was over.

The next day, it might surprise you, she was back to try again. This time the result was the same, but the back of my hand was sore. She had gotten quicker, and while she didn’t end up snapping the cards, she did slap my hand on the cards instead.

A little while later, we got to round 3. She worked out that information was key—and that was when she first became Ms. Strategic. Her new tactic was to look at her own card before putting it down. This meant that on half the occasions where a match was coming up, she knew it first. She would look at the card then move her hand down to the pile, turn it over, and snap instantly.

This strategy had me beat, at least until I found the little unconscious cue that told me she was bluffing. When Ms. Strategic had a match, her action would be much slower than otherwise, and so I became a little quicker. But it wasn’t enough. Ms. Strategic had learned to cheat. She had changed the rules of the game to suit her competitive situation. I was very proud.

We clamped down on the rule change that allowed her to look at the card after that, but let me tell you, our games of snap are far more interesting than those other parents have to endure. Moreover, my daughter can ruthlessly defeat all other children, including older ones.

Now, reading this, you might be horrified: have I created a competitive monster? But when I hear other parents complain about how boring or frustrating it is to play games with their children, I know that is the alternative. I would rather have the competition. They get to play with us more often as a result.

Of course, when it comes to some games—especially Junior Monopoly—the sheer random element, combined with the length of time needed for a game, make me want to behave quite differently. The same problem comes up with most "junior" versions of classic games. People would do well to avoid them.

Video games are a great way of playing with your children and having fun yourself. That is precisely the reason that I have trouble negotiating some gaming time with the other parent, who holds a veto on any fun.

Last summer vacation, however, a window of opportunity opened; all of a sudden, our household was overrun by video games. It all happened when my son (then six) went to play at another boy's house. His mother observed him losing dramatically in a video game we had at home but never let him play.

Clearly, he needed plenty of practice to get his skill level up. So the flood gates opened.

Basically, the six-year-old, the eight-year-old, and the thirty-six-year-old (that is, the adult with the "fun veto") were absorbed for hours and days on end at the Nintendo GameCube. That left me and the two-year-old to our own devices. Of course, a two-year-old is often amused by being handed a spare (unplugged) controller and immediately feels like an equal participant. Which left me to just watch—or quietly wander off.

One of the most popular games was Super Mario Cart: Double Dash. My son played this quite a bit. The major event occurred when he finally won a race against his older sister. This was much to our delight but not to hers, leading to tears, complaints about the intrinsic speed of the motor vehicle, and arguments about the aggregate relative allocation of time spent on these games.

I ended up consoling my daughter that, ultimately, this was all her fault. You see, in this racing game, there is an option that has one person drive while the other throws things. My daughter always took the wheel, while my son was stuck in the back throwing things. I argued that this meant he had developed those skills, while she had not. After he had finally practiced driving, he was able to tackle the race with a full arsenal—and thus he won. That was part of the story. The other part, which I also explained, was that he had caught up; and so, with a bit of luck he might win from time to time—and she would have to learn to deal with this.

Well, she dealt with it by switching games. This time to Pikmin. This was a game that obsessed our thirty-six-year-old some years back, and that obsession resurfaced. Basically, it involves a guy who crashes on a planet; in order to get off, he needs the help of little creatures called "pikmin" to gather parts and fight dangerous creatures.

Now there is a lot in the press about violent video games—anything that involves shooting, slicing open, punching, and all sorts of other things said to teach children poor behavior. These games get rated M or higher, so parents avoid them.

On the other hand, there is Pikmin. It involves cute little creatures, but to me as an observer, its message is truly horrific. Basically, the pikmin are slaves. They are bred in vast numbers just to serve the invading spaceman and help him leave the planet—a planet he leaves in ecological ruin by killing off natural predators, usually while they sleep. And this killing off is done by the pikmin, who die in vast numbers when they are unceremoniously thrown at the dangerous creatures. Some pikmin also die by "accidental" drowning; they can't swim but will blindly follow the spaceman across a pond or what have you.

I have argued that perhaps the pikmin need more respect and should have some rights—but to no avail. Instead, the thirty-six-year-old can be heard to say, "Don't worry about them, you have plenty more back on the ship." Then fifty-odd pikmin get abandoned, unprotected on the planet, only to get eaten alive or squashed.

So apparently, rampant genocide and slavery are rated G. When it comes down to it, if we are looking for games that might lead to brutal dictatorships, we should turn to Pikmin rather than Grand Theft Auto. At least the latter is localized violence, rather than the meaningless, short-term exploitation of an entire planet.

In the real world, massive multiplayer games are all the rage. If you want to wage virtual war, there are Everquest and World of Warcraft. If you want to pretend to live, there is Second Life. And for the kids, there is the torridly two-dimensional world of Club Penguin. In recent times, it has totally absorbed our family.

So what happens in the club? Basically, your kid gets a penguin (for free) and can then earn virtual coins by playing games. They can use the coins to buy things, including stuff to do up their very own igloo. They can also buy pets called puffles and spend some time trying to keep them healthy and happy. Finally, they can waddle around the world and see who else is there.

This teaches them about life. My six-year-old son played enough games to earn himself some loot and then spent it on ten puffles. He learned the lesson of over-population very quickly when he found himself unable to care for them. By the day's end, they had all passed on to another virtual place. From then on, he kept his puffle herd down.

We've told our kids not to talk to strangers. So their activities in Club Penguin are divided between saying "No!" whenever another penguin asks them to be their friend and looking for each other. So from one room someone may shout out, "Where are you?" and the response comes back, "In the Outback." Suffice it to say, the Outback is a much colder place than you would expect.

To earn coins, the kids played games. I asked whether they killed anyone, but apparently that wasn't allowed. Now how, may I ask, is this going to prepare them for other virtual games?

Typically, I would come home to this conversation:

"How long have you been playing that thing?"

"About three hours."

"Don't you think you should stop?"

"No."

"What are you doing?"

"I'm playing this ice block game. Three more rounds and I'll have enough coins to get another puffle."

"What about bath time?"

"What about it?"

"Well, the kids seem to be waiting to go to bed, and they haven't eaten since lunch. Well, except for some virtual fish."

You see, Club Penguin—like other games before it—has taken in my kids' mother. She too is obsessed with getting further in it. The entire family is now on ice.

13 Partying

There was a time when I couldn't wait for my child to have a birthday so I could plan the "bestest party ever." That lasted one birthday and one child. From then on, putting on birthday parties and taking children to birthday parties was added to my list of the costs of having children—and I put it up near the top.

I'm not alone. At one extreme, there are accounts of parties getting out of hand.[1] Kids getting picked up in limos, $600 birthday cakes, and $38,000 venue fees. Of course, this is not the norm. But, like most parents, I am pretty sure parties have become more extravagant than they ever were in our day. At the Web site Birthday Party Ideas,[2] you can see the lengths some people go to. Here, for example, is a description of an award-winning *Wizard of Oz*–themed party.

> Invitations were a tri-fold card in bright blue with yellow brick road beginning on front in a spiral, rainbow & clouds coming over top of invite, assorted flowers & pinwheels in multi-colors, with Dorothy (rubber stamp) and holding basket

> with Toto inside (made from punches), Dorothy's shoes painted with red glitter pen, the witches feet were in the bottom corner, the yellow brick continued on next page as you folded out card & you saw Glenda the Good Witch (Ellision die-cut), with flowers & pinwheels & brown fence with scarecrow, stalk of corns (all used with die-cuts & punches), the last page featured yellow brick road leading up to Emerald City (Green die cut, with green glitter paint on it) with field of poppies (made with flower punches). I bought miniature brooms & glued them to the bottom page & made a green blob out of fabric paint & put black witch hat on top, to represent the melted witch. Envelopes were in bright assorted colors & Toto die cut was used for return address, clear labels were printed on computer that said "Toto, we're not in Kansas, Anymore" and yellow brick road stamp was used underneath Toto. Address labels were printed on clear labels with a computer & they said "A party is in your future" & place inside the crystal ball rubber stamp. Invite said: "We're off to Summer's Birthday, the most wonderful 5th birthday of all. Dress as your favorite character, off to Munchkin Land we'll go. Look in your crystal ball for the date & time, you'll know." Wrote party info in silver glitter pen underneath. RSVP to Wizard himself.

Amazingly, they got past this invitation stage to pave a yellow brick road through the house, with each room decked out as a different land. And you don't want to know what went into the party favors. I was exhausted just reading about it.

To put a lid on all this, a University of Minnesota social science professor, William Doherty, launched his own Web site,

Birthdays Without Pressure.[3] As we all know, parents need restraints and boundaries, so it will draw a sympathetic audience. It even has a "pressure test" to test your own stress level when preparing for a birthday party. I was rated between 4 and 6 on the 20-point scale, which is apparently, "moderate pressure."

I must have evolved to that state, because it doesn't truly reflect my feelings. But there are a few lessons I have learned.

First, shop for party favors sensibly. I went to one of the bargain toy outlets and found a bunch of $5 educational toys and small Lego sets that were remaindered. One year I got a heap of scientific experiment kits. The parents loved it. They all put it down to my role as an educator. But in truth, it stemmed more from my being cheap.

Second, have no more than one activity per party. Parties are ridiculous if they take place at an exciting location like the zoo, but then also have a magic show and other activities. The marginal value of an extra activity is probably negative. Just don't do it.

Third, there are lots of annoying things about kids' parties. One of the biggest is that they get invited to them. What is more, the potential number of parties one child might get invited to in a year is related to, but not limited by, the number of children they have in their class. Indeed, my belief is that the biggest cost of increasing class sizes is the lost weekend time because of all the extra parties. To see what I mean, consider that with a class of twenty-four kids, you are attending a party every second weekend. If you have two children, there'll be one a week. It creates a strain. The better solution is to amalgamate parties in the class. My preferred outcome would be to nominate one day per quarter for birthdays, and then combine all the kids' parties from that quarter. I could only ever get one or two parents to go along with this, so it never happened. However, we have been able to successfully combine at least one other birthday with ours from nearby dates. It literally halves the cost of a party, and parents love it too.

Fourth, have more children. I don't mean invite more children. Instead, as you have more children of your own, the *average* extravagance of your parties will decline. This is because, by the time your second and third child arrive, you are sick of all the party planning. As a result, the events get less elaborate.

My final suggestion is to look for profit opportunities in parties. This one is nice in theory, but hard to achieve in practice. We did, however, do it once; and I believe it was a world first. Last year, my daughter became the first eight-year-old to host a Tupperware party.

Before you say "You've got to be kidding!," let me give you some background. Tupperware holds a place of high esteem in our family. My wife is an engineer. Now while that usually tends to drive her preferences against things that are, shall we say, "housewifey," Tupperware is the exception. She and a whole group of her female engineering friends have been obsessed with Tupperware for years. They held a very successful round of combined *Babylon 5*/Tupperware parties in the '90s and never looked back. And as we started to accumulate children, there was no force known that could hold back our Tupperware purchases—now they were actually likely to be of use. (We also have an obsession with Lego, that other great retail plastic brand.)

I think we own the complete Tupperware range. Our entire pantry has been Tupperwared, and if you haven't seen such things, it is an amazing sight. Moreover, we have routines dedicated to keeping the Tupperware in order. Sets together, lids in one place, other things in another. And I thought the Tupperware was meant to help us get other stuff organized! The folks at Tupperware need to develop a new meta-Tupperware product line to help us keep the Tupperware sorted out. Our current use of non-Tupperware means to this end is a travesty.

My daughter, whose preferences are not, shall we say, "girly," has inherited her mother's love of Tupperware. She has stayed up late and participated in the parties. She has learned the lore of Tupperware. I discovered today that she knows that vegetables can breathe and can tell you what setting to put broccoli on. This is all the more surprising given that she would never eat broccoli, but she is willing to tolerate it in the house because we have a specific container for it!

So that year, when we asked her what type of birthday party she wanted, it should have not come as a surprise that she wanted a Tupperware party.

Unfortunately, being pioneers, we first had to work out "What exactly is a Tupperware party for kids?" By the way, that very same question was asked by every single parent of the twelve children we invited. And, in the end, it was a cooking party.

That idea came from our Tupperware dealer. I call her a dealer because she feeds the habit. It turned out that our Tupperware dealer had thought about how to extend the franchise to a younger clientele. Like all dealers, she knew you have to get them young. She had long desired to morph her business into one where she gave cooking classes for kids, so this was the perfect opportunity for her to try out her ideas.

Now of course my daughter wanted a real Tupperware party, so we had to have the display and everyone sitting around it on chairs, looking very adult. (By the way, half of them were boys, and it was clear that this was a whole new world for them—and something they had long desired to see the inside of. They were not at all disappointed when the shroud was lifted off the Tupperware.) Then our dealer asked questions like, "What do you think you would use this for? What can you put in this square container?" (I said square fruit, which, by the way, turned out to be correct!) They played guessing games but sadly did not undertake the popular auction in which Tupperware cult members bid for little bits and pieces of plastic.

Then we moved on to the games where the children had to sort the thirteen shapes into the standard spherical Tupperware shape-sorter. (And when the audience was asked who had these when they were a child, we all put up our hands. Of course, my son pointed to his two-year-old sister and said, "She's a child and she has it now." You can't get that answer at too many other Tupperware parties.)

Then she asked if anyone knew how "Tupperware" got its name. This drew blank looks, so I chimed in. My first attempt was that it was originally made as plastic clothing. And I demonstrated how a "Bake 2 Basics Sweet Keeper" could be used as a nice hat for Melbourne Cup Day. This led to a flurry of activity as the children tried on the various bits of Tupperware. Again, something that doesn't happen at normal parties.

Apparently, I was wrong. So I gave it another shot. I argued that when he was a child, Mr. Tupper lived in a time where the fridge was unordered. People used to just toss all their fruit, vegetables, meat, and cheese into the fridge. Then they would ask their children to find various things when they needed it. Mr. Tupper's mother would shout out, "Tupper, where's the beans?" or, "Tupper, where's the sirloin." So Mr. Tupper had the idea that this would all be easier if he used plastic containers, and based on his mother's catchphrase, he decided to call it "Tupperware." This drew the response from my daughter, "Is that true?" Well, I guess not, but it turns out there was a Mr. Tupper—Earl Tupper. Who knew?

Then came the cooking, which involved making melon traffic lights with a melon ball scooper (which they each got to take home as a memento) and then cutting pizza dough into mini-pizzas with another Tupperware device (and another memento). The winning team got some prize Tupperware key rings. The food was cooked and eaten, then they were ready to go home.

Well, *they* may have been ready to go home, but round 2 in our dealer's—now nakedly transparent—plan kicked in. Various parents came by to pick the children up. Now, you wouldn't think plastic would have a distinctive smell, but it does. They flocked to the display and, half an hour later, had in vast numbers dutifully placed their orders. The total order was so large that my daughter earned about $100 in Tupperware "gifts" as a reward. She didn't choose the broccoli thing, but she now has her very own collection. And as she pointed out, "It has the distinctive feature of a lifetime guarantee, and I have a lot of life left." You didn't think of that, did you, Tupperware people?

You might like to know about the cake, and I am sure you would expect it to have been cooked in the Tupperware way.

Alas, no. My daughter wanted a *Battlestar Galactica* ice cream cake and, by the Lords of Kobol, there is no way to do that with Tupperware—they need to get a distinctive Galactica mould. So the cake was ordered, but you'll be pleased to know that it was dished out with the standard Tupperware ice cream scoop. And let me tell you, that is one effective scoop.

In summary, I can highly recommend Tupperware parties for eight-year-olds. For starters, they satisfy a deep need children have to do things that seem adult. But more important, it really is cost-effective. How many kids' parties have you run that turned a profit? And even more important, I am now the proud owner of a "special mention" at BirthdayPartyIdeas.com. I will now accept your applause. (Of course, the very act of submitting that idea caused my birthday party pressure rating to fly off the charts.)

Organizing parties is a one per child-per year affair. Taking them to parties is another matter. Here, you're lucky to get the occasional weekend off.

Sometimes it can get out of hand. Consider the following problem:

> Three missionaries and three cannibals stand on the bank of a river that they wish to cross. There is a boat available which can ferry up to two people across. The goal is to find a schedule for ferrying all the cannibals and all the missionaries safely across the river. The constraint is that, if at any point the cannibals outnumber the missionaries on either bank, the canni-

bals will eat the missionaries. Note that the boat cannot cross the river by itself with no people on board.

If you think this is just some irrelevant mind twister from school, substitute "children" for "cannibals," "parents" for "missionaries," "car" for "boat," and "across town" for "river"; then you'll have some idea of a dilemma I faced recently. Actually, the cannibal problem is better—at least there's an answer to it. That wasn't true of the situation I faced.

On that particular weekend, a (fortunately) rare event occurred. Two of our children had two parties each—on the same day and at the same times. Child No. 1 had a party at 10:30 a.m. (seeing *Shrek*), which was due to end at 1:45 p.m. and then she had another party (this time, bowling) due to begin at 1:15 p.m. and end at 3 p.m. or so. Child No. 2 had a party beginning at 10:30 a.m. and ending at 12:30 p.m. (at a park) and then another from 1 p.m. until 3 p.m. (video gaming or something). Child No. 3 had no party but really needed a nap from 1 to 3 p.m.

If you think you could have solved this, I'm not done yet. This might all be well and good if we were at the same place for all this. But of course Child No. 2's first party was at location A—twelve miles away from Child No. 1's first party, at location B. Child No. 2 then had a party at location B, while Child No. 1's second party was at location B (sort of) in terms of parking but actually a third of a mile away by foot.

To plan out at least the location side of things, I turned to Google Maps. Suffice it to say, there were real issues here. Our children's mother suggested that the problem would take a computer infinite time to solve. I said, "You think!"

Nonetheless, there needed to be a plan, so I came up with one. Clearly, I could not deposit both children at their first parties at 10:30 a.m. being, as they were, twelve miles apart. We could use the other adult in the family, but instead we tried to broker a deal with another parent, who had a child going to the same two parties as Child No. 2. The plan was this: I would take both children with me and head out from home at 9:45 a.m. We would deposit Child No. 2 at his friend's house at 10 a.m. (another thing I had to mark on the map). Sadly, this was close to his party and twelve miles or so from Child No. 1's first party. I would then drive Child No. 1 to her first party and return home. So far so good.

Now, you might think the next part of the plan would involve the other parent ferrying Child No. 2 and friend to the first and second parties. Sadly, no. As I was going to have to be at the second location in order to transfer Child No. 1 between parties there, it seemed better if I did that transfer.

So you might ask, why not find a parent to transfer Child No. 1 between her two parties? That would have freed up the middle of the day. Well, it turned out that there was *no overlap* between the kids in Child No. 1's two parties, even though they were both for kids in the same class! Why? Because the first party was a girl's party, and the second party was not. Now you might be puzzled as to how we became the only point of intersection. Well, as I noted earlier this chapter, Child No. 1, while physically a girl, is, in fact, a boy. So she gets invited to both sets of parties. The upshot of all this ridiculousness was that I had to be on site for the transfer.

But then we had another intractable issue: Child No. 1's first party ended half an hour *after* her second party began.

Something had to be thrown out, and it turned out to be Child No. 1's lunch. I would deposit Child No. 2 and friend at their second party at 1 p.m., collect Child No. 1 at 1:05 p.m., and somehow get her to the next party by 1:15 p.m. As it was a bowling party, we couldn't really be late.

From then on, the plan was that I would collect Child No. 1 at 3 p.m. while the other parent collected Child No. 2 and friend at the same time and brought them back to our house. All the while, their mother would stay with Child No. 3, who could have her nap—and so the day was solved.

I announced the plan. Then their mother piped up, "I was hoping to get a swim in today." Following that, one parent was wiped from existence.

OK, but this story isn't done yet. How did the plan go? It all looks nice and clean on Google Maps, but there are obstacles. First, there is the issue of presents. You see, not only do children have to be transported to various parties, but their presents do too. And you should never leave a child with the responsibility of transferring a present between parties; if you do, it's highly likely to get lost. Again, the missionary/cannibal issue comes up, but with a third set of things to be transported. So I needed to make contingency plans for the presents. This involved loading up the car with all of our presents and also—and I was particularly proud of myself for anticipating this one—Child No. 2's friend needed to have his present loaded into my car right at the beginning, so that I had both their presents during the crucial party 1 to 2 transfer at 12:30 p.m. What this meant was that I transported that present around all day. It failed to note the irony of this during the part of the journey when we were alone together.

Second, sometimes it is not clear what you are supposed to do with regard to parties. When I arrived at Child No. 2's first party to pick him up, I found it was a gigantic park. Where were they supposed to be? When I phoned home, I was told the invitation mentioned a pavilion at the park. It wasn't obvious where that was. So I requested support. I was expecting a high level of support, given my logistic circumstances—you know, like Jack Bauer would get in *24*.

"Call up a schematic of the park and transfer it to my PDA."

"You don't have a PDA."

"Well, my Blackberry then."

"I'm not sure I can do that."

"You know I have no room for error here."

"OK, look for a big blue building at the south end of the park, latitude 145.3188 degrees south, longitude 37.540614 degrees east."

"Got it. Thanks. Was that so hard?"

Anyhow, I went inside and found all of the children in their pajamas—apparently, some person's bright idea of a theme! Well, except one, Child No. 2. That was fine: it was winter, and he had another party to go to. But his friend was dressed like that, so we spent another five minutes trying to establish whether he had a change of clothes for his second party. Apparently not. But we were now late.

Third, there is traffic. You might think that on a Sunday, traffic isn't a problem. Not so. Location B is a traffic-and-parking disaster zone. So the last mile or so takes at least twenty minutes. During that time, traffic moves at a crawl as people try to find parking. I had finally spied a parking space on my first run into that area when someone in front of me scooted into it. I immediately took out my thumb and forefinger to apply The Force choking trick on them.

Child No. 1 commented, "Dad, you know that doesn't work outside of Star Wars."

I replied, "It works for me."

"Do they really deserve to die? They were there first."

"I'm not planning to kill them. Darth Vader just made them feel uncomfortable. Let me have my fun."

Which brings me to the final obstacle, parking. On run 1, I found a space pretty easily. But run 2 was a nightmare in this regard. We arrived ten minutes late for Child No. 2's second party and then, because I didn't want to give up my spot, I gathered up Child No. 1 and raced to her second party, arriving late for that as well. During that run I was informed that there had been a change of plans; Child No. 1 would now be collected by someone else and taken to their house, and we would pick her up later. I took the long walk back to the car and got some lunch.

At that point (while Child No. 3 had her nap, and her mother, who it turns out did survive the planning stage, went for a swim) I was able to record this memoir of that horror day.

I had done thirty miles of driving, plus a third of a mile run, and spent fully three hours in the car, and I was still not done as neither child had actually been brought safely home. Not that a failure in that regard would be totally bad (at least with regard to future parties), but the cannibals are supposed to get to the other side of the river in the correct solution to the problem.

The moral of this story is that no child should go to more than one party on any given day. It's a good rule. Let them choose who their friends really are. Otherwise, not all the missionaries are going to make it to the other side.

PART VI

THE LEARNING

14 Understanding

As an economist, I spend much of the day thinking about incentives. Throughout this book, I've shown how this has affected my parenting style. Sometimes incentives have been successful—for example, in getting the kids to eat more healthy food—while at other times they have been a dismal failure—such as our experiences with toilet training.

There are numerous things that distinguish the success stories from the failures. For starters, responding to incentives requires *ability* (hence the notion "they'll do it when they are ready"). It also requires a meaningful reward. But, perhaps most critically, using incentives requires your child to understand that a cause (some desired behavior) will lead to a future effect (a consequence). Developing that understanding is very useful, since it also allows for prediction, delayed gratification, and a number of other valuable qualities. (Of course, this presumes that such factors are not innate, which is still open to debate.)[1]

Understanding causation is a difficult challenge for children. A 2001 episode of the U.S. public radio show *This*

American Life documented stories of kid logic. This is where kids look at the evidence, use logic, and draw incorrect conclusions. They had an example of one seven-year-old child who was told by a friend, Rachel, that she knew who the tooth fairy was.

"Who was it? I have to know."

"My Dad. He is the tooth fairy."

The child ran home and told her mother.

"Mom, I know who the tooth fairy is."

"Oh, well, who is the tooth fairy?"

"Rachel's Dad is the tooth fairy!"

"I can't believe you know. It's totally secret. You can't let anyone else know. But you are right, he is the tooth fairy and he works really hard, and it's a secret."

From that day on, she believed that Rachel's Dad was the tooth fairy. What's more, her parents played along by signing his name on notes left under her pillow. It took a few years before both children worked out the truth that sure, he was the tooth fairy, but it was all much more tooth than fairy.

Our family has a story like this, too. When Child No. 1 was four, she revealed to me that her mother controlled the traffic lights. I found this out while we were stopped at a light, waiting for it to turn green, and I uttered some complaint. She told me that if Mom were here, she could simply change the light so we could go.

I probed a bit to find out why this was the case.

"Well, her car has a stick that if you move it down and press that pedal, the light turns green. Your car doesn't have that."

Ah ha. So what had been happening was this. Her mother—who enjoys feeling like she's driving a Ferrari—had a small manual car. When the light turned green, she would whip into gear right away, and off they would go. To my daughter, these events were virtually simultaneous. So she formed the view that it was the gear shift that caused the light change, rather than the other way around. (I asked her when she was eight whether she still believed this, but she doesn't. She does remember that she did once think so but has rewritten her memory to suggest that her mother claimed it was so.)

The two stories have something in common.[2] In both cases, the child attributed superhuman qualities to the parent. That they should do this is amusing to us, but, in fact, it takes some time for children to work out which of their parents' magical abilities are normal rather than special. But the two stories are also separated by an element of conspiracy. While my daughter may have simply had an overdeveloped appreciation of her mother's importance in the world, in the other story, the causal myth (the tooth fairy—which I'll come back to later) was a construction that the parents conspired to maintain by filtering the evidence.

I'll tell you right now, I have no magic formula for how to establish an understanding of cause and effect. All I know is, if a child doesn't have it, parenting efforts based on causal understanding are doomed to fail.

When my son was two, he had a little doll's stroller. It was small, but he could fit into it. So in he got, and his older sister pushed him around. We snapped some pictures of how cute they looked. Then he tried to get out.

BAM! He fell straight, face first, onto the hard wood floor. Blood was spurting everywhere, from his mouth and nose. And it was as painful as it sounds. He was distraught. All cuteness left the scene; photography was out and triage was in.

Now, one reaction to all of this would have been: "How about we take away that dangerous toy?" But did we do this? No. Our reasoning was that he had learned his lesson. Surely, given the pain it caused, he would never get in the thing again.

Perhaps you're thinking that a few days later he tried his luck again. There is a sense in which I could live with that. But sadly, that wasn't to be.

Instead, no sooner had we cleaned up the blood and calmed him down to the point where he was happy to go off and play again, he got straight back in the stroller! What he was thinking I don't know. Somehow he had not established the connection between getting into the stroller and the trauma getting out of it. Perhaps we needed to take some pictures of him bloody and crying. Suffice it to say, he didn't get another chance to learn that particular lesson; now he would have to carry his baby doll around until he grew up.

Child No. 2's understanding of the world has improved markedly since then, but he does tend to live for the moment. According to a recent school report (from first grade), "He tends to lose track of his possessions, but that doesn't faze him one bit." He is aware of future consequences but, at the same time, places little weight on them. There will be only so much incentives can do there.[3]

Standing in complete contrast is Child No. 1. She places an enormous weight on future consequences. For instance, she can't stand the idea that someone at the dinner table will still be eating dessert when she doesn't have any left. So she waits until her siblings have almost finished before starting her own.

Sometimes, to torture her, I delay my dessert too (if I'm allowed any) to see whether she will "break" and go first. This is not a game I can win. Turns out she is far more patient than I am, and we both end up with ice cream soup, something she plainly likes more than I do.

These same qualities have given her a strategic mindset. Recently, she had a swimming "race" night. This is a monthly event at her swimming school at which the kids are timed and get a ribbon if they get their personal best (or PB, as it is called by Olympians). This was my daughter's first race night, so she would get a ribbon regardless of how well she performed.

She swam the 25- and 50-meter races in all of her strokes, but surprisingly slowly. I thought she was just tired. But after the short races, she would bound back up to the starting end of the pool. She clearly still had energy to burn, so it didn't add up.

Afterward, I asked her how she felt about it all.

"Good."

"But didn't you think you were a little slower than usual?'

"Oh that's true. I wanted a slow time."

"Why?"

"Well, then I won't have as much to beat next month, so I can get another PB."

There is actually an economic term for this phenomenon: *the ratchet effect*. This arises when your future performance targets are based on your past performance. They constantly ratchet up. It creates an incentive to hold back and reduce today's performance so that tomorrow's target is easier to attain.

So when you want a ribbon every month, it is best not to fall into the trap of over-performance. One good month and you pay for it forever. My daughter realized that, so it didn't bother her at all when she came in last. The rest of the children in her races were going to pay for the error next month. And as long as rewards are based on individual rather than relative performance, my daughter will continue to engage in leisurely races.

Suffice it to say, her plan to accumulate ribbons didn't quite work out. We haven't been invited to a race night since.

It is not just understanding the link between a current action and a future reward or punishment that creates incentives; context plays a role, too. Just to remind us that incentives are not all about rational economics, let's consider nontangible rewards—such as praise. It turns out that if you praise a child all the time, it loses effectiveness.

Another serious problem with praise was demonstrated in an experiment led by psychologist Carol Dweck.[4] She took schoolchildren out of their classrooms for a simple nonverbal IQ test. After they completed it, a random sample of children were praised for their intelligence, while others were praised for their effort. The children were then given another test and allowed to choose between an easy and a hard version. The type of praise they'd been given affected their choices. Ninety percent of those praised for effort took the hard path, while the majority of the others took the easy route.

In the next round, no child had a choice. They each got a very difficult test. Interestingly, the children who had been praised for their effort tried harder, not stopping until they had explored all avenues. The "intelligent" children gave up earlier. Finally, they were all given an easy puzzle, like the one at the start. The "effort" children's performance rose by 30 percent while the "smart" children's performance actually *fell* by 20 percent.

> Dweck had suspected that praise could backfire, but even she was surprised by the magnitude of the effect. "Emphasizing effort gives a child a variable that they can control," she explains. "They come to see themselves as in control of their success. Emphasizing natural intelligence takes it out of the child's control, and it provides no good recipe for responding to a failure."

It is so easy to praise performance without thinking. I used to do it all the time. But what studies like this show is that it can become not only a blunt instrument but a destructive one unless it's used carefully. Incentives work when children (and others) can actually adjust their behavior. If you praise someone for an innate ability, they have no such control. But if you praise them for something they can control, that's another matter. Then the rewards can work.

Similarly, children seem adept at working out when incentives are present and when they are absent—for precisely the same behavior. We discovered this at Child No. 1's third grade parent-teacher interview. It began:

"I have to tell you that your child is a delight."

"Really?'

"Yes, she does everything she is told. She is always ready at the beginning of class, with her ry on the table. She works hard all day at projects. And she always helps clean up."

"Umm, we're the *Gans* family; G-A-N-S. Take another look at your sheet. Are we talking about the same child?"

Turns out that we *were* talking about the same child—physically, at least. At home, "compliant" is not the word I would use for Child No. 1. Sure, faced with the inevitable, she is very good and does most things without being reminded. But to get her to do anything extra is a real struggle—she clearly believes that if she complies, she might be stuck doing whatever distasteful activity it is for the rest of her life. Actually, she is probably right about that.

Nonetheless, let's face it, we can't complain. If we are going to have compliance somewhere, best that it be at school. Indeed, we rewarded that by allowing her to have more of a free reign with her time at home.

But I was curious. Why was there such a difference? We asked her about it.

"Well, of course I'm well behaved. They pay me there."

"What do you mean?"

"We get money. Well, not real money, but bonus money. I have the most in the class."

Ah ha! Yet again she proves to be her father's daughter. At school, they must get the incentives right, which is clearly not the case at home. She understood the difference and reacted accordingly. Nonetheless, I don't think we are going to change things here, lest we upset the current happy situation at school.

While understanding cause and effect can be the key to most incentives foisted on children, sometimes we try to obscure an understanding of the truth to achieve a similar end. After all, if Santa Claus and the list of "good boys and girls" isn't an artificially created incentive system, I don't know what is!

A little while back, I spent considerable energy thinking about the tooth fairy. It was our own fault really. One day, Child No. 1 lost her sixth tooth. The next morning, she woke up to tell us that the tooth fairy hadn't come. That was when the trouble started.

My initial reaction to this sad news was to go up and check her "tooth box," carrying money in my hand in a vain attempt to suggest that she had just missed it, being bleary eyed in the morning. This plan was aborted when I opened the box to find, well, a tooth. To take the tooth now would be a tad too obvious.

On to plan B: imaginative lying. We settled on, "Obviously, lots of children must have lost teeth yesterday, and the tooth fairy is just one fairy and can only do so much. She will be here tonight." Our daughter bought that and, indeed, when discussing the incident with a friend, it turned out the same thing had happened to him once, and he got the same explanation. (We must remember to thank his parents!)

A colleague of mine told me about his own "imaginative lie" when faced with a similar dilemma. He said to his daughter (and I am not making this up), "Oh, I came into your room last night and saw a bright thing buzzing around that looked like a firefly, and so I swatted it." It wasn't clear whether he killed it or just frightened it away, but his daughter was suitably (and understandably) horrified.

In light of that, our lie was much more tame. However, that didn't stop another parent from being horrified as I recounted the day's incident: "How could you just lie to your children?" Ahem, it is the "tooth fairy" we're talking about here! I think I have pretty much free license on that one.

To continue the story, we almost forgot again the next night, but remembered just in time. But we have so many more teeth to come and go among our three children that this is bound to be an ongoing issue.

Which led me to rethink the whole tooth fairy thing. From an efficiency standpoint, it would be much better if a child could simply present a tooth to us and receive cash on the spot. No running around at midnight searching for coins and teeth. It also saves on other inefficiencies. This time around, our daughter ended up with New Zealand currency (I had just returned from there and found some lying about). When she asked about that, I embellished the original lie. "The Australian tooth fairy has been busy, as you know, so she probably asked the New Zealand one to come and help her out." Just one more example of globalization working for the greater good.

But how did we end up in our current situation? According to Wikipedia, the tooth fairy originated in the United States around 1900. But the idea really appears to have taken off in Western cultures since World War II. Why? Wikipedia's suggestions allude to the value of myth and how much children like storytelling. But that doesn't ring true.

When it comes down to it, I think my daughter knows exactly where the money is coming from, but she is quite happy to "play the tooth fairy game," if only for the benefit of her younger siblings. So there is no sense of wonderment there. Just the usual raw economic calculus.

My hypothesis is that the "tooth fairy deal" persists because it is an excellent incentive device. When a child has a loose tooth, there is a possibility that it may not come out on its own, necessitating more drastic action. This might be a parental intervention (you know, the string and the door trick), or worse, an expensive trip to the dentist. Unless the child endures a little bit of pain and wiggles the loose tooth. To give them an incentive, we offer some money for the tooth. Giving them a dollar or two rather than, say, $50 to the dentist, seems like a good deal.

Indeed, we know of a child who was booked to go to the dentist in a couple of days' time but was offered (and it is not quite clear how this fits in with the tooth fairy lie) $20 if they could pop the tooth that day. Surprise, surprise, that is just what happened. I pity those parents; however, what will happen with the next tooth? The child will anticipate the dentist deal and wait until the last minute. Much better to toe a strict tooth fairy line.

This led me to think more about the other economic issues associated with tooth fairies. For instance, how do you set a price on teeth? Our policy is this: the price is some proportion (perhaps 100 percent) of the change I happen to be carrying. On my very first night as an agent of the fairy, I realized that whatever we paid this time might affect future payment amounts. Moreover, the effect could only be inflationary. If I didn't have the correct change, I might be tempted to up the deal. Anyway, we paid $1 for the first tooth and went on from there.

On the second tooth, Child No. 1 got less. On the third tooth she got more. In each case, it was explained that the amount was set by the tooth fairy—and there was no reason to expect her to be consistent.[5]

The beauty of this strategy is that every time one of the children loses a tooth, we don't have to think. No need to worry about what the last payment was, what other children got, and so on. And let me tell you, we need less of this type of thinking in our lives. We can just delve into our pockets, pull out an amount, and go from there. This frees us of much of the mess associated with tooth financial management. We simply floated the tooth exchange rate to free up management effort for more important areas.

15 Schooling

I am going to start this penultimate chapter with a Seinfeldesque rant. What is the deal with all the reading? It seems that as soon as we work out a child can see, we thrust letters in their face, read them books, carefully pointing out the words so they know we're not making it up, and then, when they get to school, we count down the days to literacy.

I am not an innocent bystander in all this fuss. We did everything we could to get Child No. 1 to read. When she was just two (now this may sound completely ridiculous, but it wasn't at the time), we labeled everything in the house using the pretty Comic Sans font. Visitors were astonished but soon appreciated the fact that they could easily find the bathroom. It was at least three more years before Child No. 1 made much of the signs.

We learned our lesson and had lightened up by the time Child No. 1 got to school. But that didn't end her struggles, and it pained me to watch. Learning to read English is excruciating. It is a tough activity, and, what is more, the case for expecting kids to be reading at six rather than by eight is not particularly strong. In Scandinavian countries, they don't begin formal training until the age of seven.

Sure, some kids can read by age four (we have one), and it means they can do lots more things. But they are also reading by that age because those are the things they are interested in. Forcing others to fit that mold may not be useful. If you factored out natural ability, I'm not sure whether early reading would lead to improved academic performance later. But, right at the start of school, reading is Job No. 1, and the pressure is significant.

All this gets reinforced by a desire to teach "a love of books." Now I am not one to rail against books; I'm an academic after all, and I am writing one now. But the hard sell of books by teachers and many authors is really a bit much. I was once dragged to a special meeting for all parents in Child No. 1's class. The teacher explained that not all children learn to read at the same rate (fair enough), but that it was critical we read to them at home. What I heard then was that if your child wasn't reading, it wasn't the teacher's fault—but it might be yours. In truth, it's unlikely that blame could be apportioned so easily. Indeed, is there any need to cast blame at all?

The theory of school education is that objective practitioners will carefully implement a curriculum that is designed to elicit maximal learning, alongside social development, to the long-term benefit of all. But in practice, schools are as much a product of society as they are a producer. At almost every turn, parental pressure drives what is taught at school and how it is taught. As an educator myself, I have watched this over the years with increasing frustration, and I will rail about it here as

I consider the three interfaces for the school and parents: homework, parent-teacher conferences, and theatrical disasters.

Before I had children of school age, I watched with interest the rising tide against homework. The idea was that children (especially those under ten) had too much homework at night. Well, the academic in me said "What rot! Work is good." And I awaited the day when one of my own children would be assigned homework.

Well, that happened when my eldest daughter was in her first year of school, and it started with "The Readers." This was an endless parade of little books designed to encourage children to gain confidence in reading. Every night, several of these would come home, and every night we would struggle through them. Each time, I would wonder: isn't this what they should be doing at school?

It took us two years, but we finally fought back. We simply said "no." If we were going to spend half an hour a night on educational activities, it was going to be stuff I didn't think she was getting at school—and stuff she would do enthusiastically. So we switched to math activity books with "word problems." This encouraged her to read and to solve problems—two hits for the price of one. As far as I could tell, she wasn't doing these types of things at school. It also made our lives considerably easier.

Homework needs a rationale and a goal. Doing it for its own sake is counterproductive, especially if your child doesn't like the activity. This was exactly our rationale in substituting reading for math. And it turns out that homework only has observable impacts on performance when it is very targeted. That seems to be the logic behind the list of spelling words we rehearse every night, which tends to result in them being learned.

But even so, I worry that the total volume of work time after school—piano (fifteen minutes), spelling (ten minutes), project or math (thirty minutes)—is still too much for a seven-year-old. Especially since our kids attend after-school care most days and on other days have piano or swimming lessons. That just leaves the weekend for any simple, do-whatever-you-want play time. Sure, that is what it's like for adults all the time—but that isn't much of an argument.

So, how did we get into this situation? Well, we do extracurricular activities because we choose to. And we could (superficially) blame the schools for the rest. But, actually, I suspect that we (or at least, other parents) are at fault. It is parents who ask the teachers for more work and then use homework to judge school performance. Not surprisingly, it is easy to send students home with more work, just to shut the parents up.

For that reason, I am inclined to ignore school-directed homework and instead choose our own activities. But it is difficult to know how long we will be able to keep that up in today's competitive world.

The next item on my list of parental involvement in school life is the parent-teacher conference. Apparently, many parents do not think these are useful. So much so that Texas is considering making parent-teacher meetings mandatory. Parents who don't show up would be fined.

There are two reactions to this. First, what makes parent-teacher interviews so painful that you won't show up? Second, what use are they anyway? Let me deal with each of these questions in turn.

Something that I didn't expect when becoming a parent is that I would dread parent-teacher conferences. Now, you are obviously assuming that the main reason for this is that we are greeted with a long list of problems about our children. That would make sense—if it were true. Instead, as I mentioned in the last chapter, from our perspective they are better characterized as a "love fest" (mostly). I actually don't think this is because our children are incredibly special. It is just that there are no longstanding problems that are not dealt with at other times. If there is a real issue, and there have been a few, the teacher does not wait until the parent-teacher meeting to let us know about it. An immediate phone call at work or right after school is the order of the day. So we go into these conferences expecting the love fest.

The issue is this. As a university lecturer, I sympathize with teachers in their dealings with students. As a lecturer to MBAs, I sympathize with teachers and their dealings with parents (MBA students can be tough customers). For a teacher, having to deal with parents opens them up to criticism. They face the same issues I do—first and foremost, trying to remember who the student is and whether there have been any past issues. How can they expect to know this?

Actually, at preschool and primary school, teachers do a pretty good job of remembering who students are. For specialist classes, that drops off; I have sat in discussions with a music teacher where they are clearly winging it. That actually amuses me, so those are fine but ultimately useless.

So when we go to these meetings, both of us sit there mute. I feel like we are drooling, and I definitely get the impression that the teacher is thinking, "Are these really this child's parents?" I just do not know what to say. I don't want to be pushy. I am happy to hear good things. And I rarely have any sort of agenda.

The teacher doesn't know what to do with us. They look for a fight. They expect to have to write down an action list. But, in the end, there is nothing like that. We go away thinking how awkward it all was and wondering whether we should have had an agenda. Indeed, we try to come up with a few trivial concerns for next time. Things like, Child No. 1 is having trouble finishing her lunch on time; can you allocate a few more minutes to that? Child No. 2 thinks there is too much time for lunch and he gets bored sitting there. Perhaps then we could really achieve something.

So I can understand why parents might not like to turn up to these things at all. But that is a different thing from making them show up.

The question is: what is the purpose of this conference? With more continuous communication between parents and teachers throughout the semester, the real problems are addressed elsewhere. Emily Bazelon outlined the idea of a "three-way conference."[1]

> The parent-teacher conference can serve to reinforce the enmity, especially if it takes parents back to their own miserable

school days. (Those little chairs are nothing if not infantilizing.) The conference can also cut through the adversarial posturing—especially, perhaps, if it takes the form of a three-way conversation: teacher, parent, and kid. Lawrence-Lightfoot thinks this should be the rule, not the exception. And not just for older students. She has seen six-year-olds talk about themselves at a conference with "insight and discernment."

I ran this idea by my sister, a doctoral student in education at the University of Pennsylvania who taught for five years at a public school in the Bronx and at a charter school in Los Angeles. She liked it. From a teacher's perspective, conferences are useful because they push you to reflect on each kid and her schoolwork. To go through a child's portfolio with her, and talk together about her academic progress and behavior, would be all the more meaningful. And if the teacher needs the parents' help with an unruly child, "It's definitely better for the student to be there," my sister said. There's no confusion about who's saying what. Plus, the only people who know what the child is like both at school and at home are present, not absent.

One study of four schools with conferences that included students, by Diana Hiatt-Michael of Pepperdine University, found close to 100 percent parent participation.

Our school instituted this last year for Child No. 2 in kindergarten, but (ironically) I missed it because of work commitments. Anyhow, by all accounts, it didn't really serve any function at that age. Everyone talked about what Child No. 2

needed to improve, including Child No. 2, but there was no information really exchanged. Maybe it will be more useful for children older than five.

The key issue for me is: who is supposed to be learning what? The parent learns little about the children at these things (that usually occurs at other times). The parent learns a bit about the teacher, but the bilateral nature of these conferences suggests that it would be more efficient to have a group session where a bunch of parents meet the teacher.

So the only thing left is for the teacher to learn more about the parents. And there are good reasons for this to be important. Let's face it, getting to know the parents and perhaps the siblings would be the best way for a teacher to understand the circumstances of the child, especially for younger children. However, our conferences are not ideal for that.

First, they take place in the teacher's domain—the classroom. With the parents out of context, not much can be learned. Personally, I give away nothing. I'm sure that teachers get the impression that little conversation goes on in our household—and that we do lots of smiling and nodding.

Second, the teachers are not interrogating the parents. They are usually reporting to them. The flow of information is not in the right direction.

Finally, most parents would not welcome an interrogation. Let's face it, this isn't going to increase participation. However, such conferences might prove more useful in the form of home visits by the teacher. I am pretty sure we'd be just as happy to sit there mute in the comfort of our own home, but the teacher might be able to glean a little information from our surroundings.

Then again, I am also pretty sure we'd have a new issue—getting teachers to participate! It is like a waterbed. Push down on one issue and another pops up in its place. But then again, performance evaluation is always like that.

Now on to the final touching point: the annual public exhibit of children's theatrical prowess. At our school, we have "Dance Night." At this annual event, the kindergartners and first graders, and their families, are crammed into a large gymnasium. The event consists of an assortment of songs sung by children and dances danced by children, all to the tune of whirring camcorders. Families jockey for position to zoom in on their moving child, trying to isolate them from the other hundred children doing the same thing. If I ever missed one of these events and had to watch it on video, my experience would be much the same. I don't think I have seen a child perform except through a camcorder screen! That's all I ever see.

Anyhow, the first dance is, of course, prior to the show as the experienced parents (those with older children) stake out the best locations. They then watch with amusement as the inexperienced ones flounder. This is particularly fun at our school, since the best locations are not where you would think. Experienced parents head up high to the gallery so they can look down on the events and also pick out their child from above. They then watch the inexperienced parents jumping for joy as they find front row seats on the gymnasium floor. Those parents then observe us up high and wonder what we are all doing there when we could get a seat so close to the action.

Little do they know. A few smart ones work out the difference between us and them and switch (which is what we did our first time). But many do not; or even more amusingly, one parent argues for switching while the other doesn't want to, in a wonderful hint of foreboding.

Then the fun really begins. When the children start performing, the parents in the front row realize they can't see their particular child. Dozens of others are in front. Then they want to stand, but of course they cannot, because there are parents behind them. A few more flee to the gallery, but by then it is too full. Their thoughts turn to next year, when they will have a better plan.

Now to the actual show. I have formed the view that the standard by which to judge children's concerts is not how competent they are—but, instead, how *in*competent they are. Incompetence is a good thing. Competence is bad. The reason is this: these shows will never contain objectively good performances (you know, the kind that you would pay to see even if they didn't involve a loved one). There is always some hopeful music teacher conducting passionately down the front, chin in the air, with a clear "pain of hopefulness" expression that can never quite be relieved. A group of young children simply can't get it together that well.

Instead, the aim for us as parents is to get some amusement value from the whole event. I didn't quite realize this until the second time I attended. This is because the first was so darned hilarious. At that first event, Child No. 1 could not help but move her arms to the music, and even got in a bit of air guitar. In a choir full of children standing stock still with their arms by their sides, this was intensely amusing to me and made for one great video.

But it got even better. When it came to the dancing, my daughter's irregular habit was a sign of competence. Now you would think that, by my metric, this would have destroyed my enjoyment. Not so. This is because this was the sort of dancing that involved another child. And this boy had the requisite characteristics for fun.

My daughter's dance "partner" was, shall we say, uninterested. Unlike my daughter, the whole concept of moving was not really his thing. He wasn't against it, but he was clearly not going to expend much effort. My daughter had clearly worked this out already from their practice sessions and was ready to do whatever it took. Basically, she handled him physically (she was quite a bit taller) and literally pushed or outright placed him where he had to be. If he had to kneel, he was pushed down. If he had to stand, he was pulled up. If he had to move around the circle, he was herded. If he had to spin around, he was swung. It was by far the funniest thing I have ever seen.

Which brings me back to my hypothesis on incompetence. The next year, it was round 2 for my daughter as she moved to first grade. Imagine my thrill when I heard she would be partnered with the very same boy as last year!

But sadly, everyone had become much, much better. The songs were sung without movement, and the dances were executed without drama. The boy had become interested enough not to require special attention. And all the amusement value was gone.

So it was with great anticipation that we moved on to Child No. 2 and back to potential incompetence. Our expectation was that he would be the uninterested boy that we had loved two years earlier. I was very optimistic.

Unfortunately, the school administrators had decided that the grueling one-and-a-half-hour performance with no break was a bit much. They had scaled things back to a light sixty minutes, with lots of alternating breaks for individual classes. Moreover, the routines and songs were extremely tame. It was all brought back to the children's level of competence, so that is what we got. As a result, it was no fun at all.

To get an enjoyable performance from children, you need two elements. First, an ambitious program, unmatched to the children's ages. The children must be set up to fail. Long, difficult dances. Plays with lots of hard words. No chance that anyone can hope to memorize them.

Second, the children need lots of practice, so that it looks like there was a serious attempt to do it right. But not years of learning.

Add these two ingredients together, and you get to the edge of competence. That is the only thing that will give you cherished video memories.

PART VII

THE TIME

16 Continuing

When my PhD thesis advisor, Ken Arrow, found out that I was soon to have my first child, he said to me, "Just remember, it is an investment." He was referring to the difficulties parents face during those first few years; but I suspect that, through the luck of the draw, his own experience had been tougher than the norm. Still, it is important to remind yourself that the job can be a difficult one, with payoffs well into the future.

There is a famous *Peanuts* comic that appears in most economics textbooks (including mine). Charlie Brown is watching the news, and there are reports like: "Skies were sunny today, but economists warn that this could cause an increase in the price of sunglasses." And it's funny because it's true. Economists, as a group, tend to focus a lot on the costs of various activities. Here, I have spent considerable time highlighting the costs of parenting.

Interestingly, I haven't focused on the monetary costs at all—you know, the hundreds of thousands of dollars parents will forgo in lifetime wealth as a result of having one or more children. Instead, the costs I've concerned myself with are the personal ones: dealing with a lack of sleep, getting children to eat, toileting, washing hands, sharing, getting on planes, staying on planes, eating at restaurants, dealing with parties, and so on.

Shane Greenstein, an economics professor at Northwestern's Kellogg School of Management, who has four children of his own, came up with what he affectionately terms "the four losses of parenting." They are:

With child number one, you lose your time.

With child number two, you lose your money.

With child number three, you lose your ideals.

With child number four, you lose your home office.

For other people, these losses might manifest themselves with different children. For our part, we definitely lost our time with Child No. 1, and we lost money as our household income fell to accommodate Child No. 2. When Child No. 3 came long, we lost a room but also our ideals. Limiting TV watching and treats, time spent reading to our children, time spent reading about our children, time spent keeping abreast of what they're doing at school, and time spent knowing where they are and what they're doing. All these were core values that flew out the window as the number of children accumulated. So we're all high and mighty until the costs rise, and then it turns out we couldn't care less. The sad thing is, the compromise occurred for far less than we ever expected at the outset.

In many respects, my perspective may seem like a selfish one; that is also an economist's trait. But these are the things we deal with on a day-to-day basis. They are the reason why psychologists such as Harvard's Daniel Gilbert have found that while most of us claim that "children make us happy," the years when we are actually caring for children don't rate as happy ones for most parents.[1] But I guess it's the thought that counts.

Of course, being upfront about the personal costs associated with parenting doesn't deny the overwhelming benefits that also arise. However, the benefits seem more difficult to measure.

As a parent, the hardest thing to do is to set goals. No, I don't mean goals for your children, I mean goals for you as parents. You need a goal in order evaluate whether you are doing well or doing badly relative to that goal. In business terms, the closest analogue is the "vision statement."

Vision statements can be useless or useful. The useless ones are invariably too broad ranging. They set goals such as "We are going to be No. 1." Now that's all very well, but it doesn't tell you what you're *not* going to be—and that is something you need to know, because you can't do everything. Useful vision statements place more emphasis on what you aren't going to do. For instance, one of the world's most consistently profitable companies, Lincoln Electric, has this motto: "Once we're in, we never lose a sale except on delivery." This sounds strange, but it's useful. Lincoln's emphasis is on quality, but this sometimes means they have to compromise on delivery times. So occasionally, they lose out to others because of that.

The same applies to parenting. You can set a goal to teach your children to be the "best they can be." But then you are setting yourselves and probably them (in your eyes) up for failure. As novelist Orson Scott Card put it:[2]

> Why in the world should we ever, ever ask any child to *be* the best at anything? Or try to guess when they have *done* their best? Why is that even our job, as parents?
>
> That's *their* job—to decide what they want to do, and then decide when they've done all they can (or want) in order to excel at that task.
>
> For instance, why should someone even aspire to be the best doctor? Why not aspire to be a *good* doctor? If they aim to be the *best*, they can never succeed, because even if, miraculously, they are the best in their profession for a brief moment, they will age, and some young whippersnapper will come along and do better.

Superficially, being "the best" sounds like a good goal, but it doesn't stand up to closer scrutiny. The goal of being happy also has its downsides. After all, we seem to want our children to have a happy childhood, but we also want them to be able to deal with life outside the home—and sometimes that involves leaving them open to some frustration and personal hardship.

When we were expecting Child No. 1, at one point we started to panic. What are we doing here? How will we know if we're doing a good job? We had simply not thought things through. We needed a vision statement to work it out.

In the end, our vision statement was simple: when we looked back thirty or so years from now, we would consider our parenting job a failure if our children had not become independent adults. That was it. We have no definitions for success, just a single, subjective criterion for failure. The moral philosophy behind this is also simple: we don't want our children to be a burden on society. (Now if, due to health problems, full independence did not occur, that would be another matter; here we are talking about the normal course of events.)

This vision statement isn't for everyone. When we came up with it, it seemed right for us—but how could we know for sure? Maybe it would not work for anyone other than us. But we find it incredibly useful. We come back to it all the time, whenever we're agonizing over decisions and dilemmas. By having a vision, and one defining a clear risk of failure, we have given ourselves both comfort and a challenge. My point here is that this vision statement is reflected in our choices and colors my perspective in this book.

For us, this isn't the end of the story, even if it is the end of this book. The situations I have raised have all come from experiences with children aged minus-three months to eight years old. And it turns out that once you start being a parent, it never ends. It is just that the situations and problems change.

As you might have gathered, being an economist gives me a certain perspective on issues I face as a parent. In some cases, that perspective helps—for instance, in working out how to negotiate with children over food and sleep and being able to cope with my specialized roles in the delivery room and the classroom. In other cases, the economist in me has not helped matters. Economic incentives did nothing to speed up toileting, even if economic theory understood why those techniques failed. I have no magic ways of keeping children safe or organizing my way out of parties. But economics does help me to see all the costs involved.

The good news for me is that, apparently, little else helps either. If your goal is to raise a high academic achiever, what appears to matter is what type of people you actually *are* rather than what type of parents you might try to be. In *Freakonomics*, Steve Levitt looked at a dataset of twenty thousand American schoolchildren and what their parents did for them. Those who were ferried around to heaps of activities, taken to museums on the weekend, had a parent stay at home in the early years, or were not allowed to watch TV did not perform any better than their counterparts who missed out on all that stuff.

The sobering fact is that there are only a few broad things you can do as a parent to influence the life of your children beyond the home. The rest of parenting is about managing the day-to-day stuff. To be sure, when a child chooses to, say, eat with their fingers at dinner, this may upset both you and others. However, the real issue is not a child choosing to do that per se, but whether they have made their choice at least taking into account its impact on others. If so, it is not purely selfish in my eyes and bodes well for the future—at times when their own pleasure does not exceed the costs they impose on others.[3] But it is a work in progress.

I have seen the awareness of such costs evolve within my own children. But it has always emerged in a way that reflects their own innate characters. For example, I have one child who thinks things are unfair if someone gets more than her, but another who thinks things are unfair if someone gets less than him. And then I have a third who, at the moment, has large cheeks and deep dimples that have given her a license not to care about whether something is fair or not. She will eventually care, I know that.

The core message here is that, in preparing children to become part of society, parents have a role in showing their children how what they do affects others. A parent's own behavior, their communication about what is right and what is wrong, and their explanation of all of the costs and benefits associated with a child's actions all add to the mix. It enables kids to make choices for themselves and start to do things that at least appear to rise above their own self-interest. Then, when they're ready, they can go out on their own.

Notes

Preface

1. Game Theorist at http://gametheorist.blogspot.com.
2. Economists have studied parenting before, but they are usually more concerned with issues of why people become parents, and what drives how many children they have (see, for example, Greg J. Duncan and Katherine A. Magnuson, "Economics and Parenting," mimeo, Northwestern University, 2002). In contrast, the present volume deals with the day-to-day minutia of being a parent.

Chapter One

1. In Taiwan, there are certain days when it is lucky to have a child, so births are moved to those days (J. C. Lo, "Patient Attitudes vs. Physicians' Determination: Implications for Cesarean Sections," *Social Science and Medicine* 57 (2003): 91–96). Also, when it came to the Millennium, parents opted to delay births until after January 1, 2000 (see Joshua Gans and Andrew Leigh, "The Millennium Bub," *Applied Economics*, forthcoming).
2. See Joshua Gans and Andrew Leigh, "Bargaining Over Labour: Do Patients Have Any Power?" *Discussion Paper*, Melbourne Business School, 2006.

3. An even clearer example of this comes when you examine what happens to birth rates during the week of annual obstetrics conferences. The birth rate falls on those dates by a statistically significant amount (around 2 percent in the United States and 4 percent in Australia). See Joshua Gans, Andrew Leigh, and Elena Varganova, "Minding the Shop: The Case of Obstetrics Conferences," *Social Science and Medicine* 65, no. 7 (2007): 1458–1465.
4. Stacey Dickert-Conlin and Amitabh Chandra, "Taxes and the Timing of Births," *Journal of Political Economy* 107, no. 1 (1999): 161–177.
5. Daniel Leonhardt, "To-Do List: Wrap Gifts. Have Baby," *New York Times*, December 20, 2006.
6. *7:30 Report*, Australian Broadcasting Corporation, July 1, 2004.
7. All this is documented in Joshua Gans and Andrew Leigh, "Born on the First of July: An (Un)natural Experiment in Birth Timing," *Journal of Public Economics* (2008, forthcoming).
8. Actually, this might not be as crazy as it sounds. Google Trends shows a spike in queries in Australia for "plasma televisions" at the same time as a spike for queries on "Baby Bonus."

Chapter Two

1. http://www.poly.rpi.edu/article_view.php3?view=4918&part=1
2. Indeed, if you have lots of babies and/or long labors and so need lots of material, I can also recommend Tony Martin's *Lolly Scramble* or anything by Bill Bryson as good delivery-room fare.

Chapter Three

1. J. Martin and M. Wake, "Adverse Associations of Infant and Child Sleep Problems and Parent Health: An Australian Population Study," *Pediatrics* 119, no. 5 (May 2007): 947–955.
2. Of course, this suggests, as economist Barry Nalebuff did to me, that parents should spend their scarce money not on day care, but on night care. They could hire someone to come a few nights a week to be the designated first stop for an awake baby. That person would determine if some feeding was required and then wake a parent as a last resort. This might be enough to keep the parents sane—money well

spent. See also Eilene Zimmerman, "Baby Cries at 2 A.M.? No Need to Get Up," http://www.nytimes.com/2008/07/13/jobs/13starts.html.

3. C. Green, *Toddler Taming* (Sydney: Doubleday, 1990), 119.

4. According to the *Telegraph* ("Babies not as innocent as they pretend," July 1, 2007), Dr. Vasudevi Reddy at the University of Portsmouth has found that infants use fake crying or pretend laughing to win attention (http://www.telegraph.co.uk/earth/main.jhtml?xml=/earth/2007/07/01/scibaby101.xml).

5. Richard Ferber, *Solve Your Child's Sleep Problems* (New York: Fireside, 1986).

6. http://www.slate.com/id/2166888

7. Brie A. Moore, Patrick C. Friman, Alan E. Fruzzetti, and Ken MacAleese, "Brief Report: Evaluating the Bedtime Pass Program for Child Resistance to Bedtime—A Randomized, Controlled Trial," *Journal of Pediatric Psychology* 32, no. 3 (2007): 283–287.

Chapter Four

1. See for instance, the "Economic Benefits of Breastfeeding," put out by the U.S. Breastfeeding Committee (an advocacy group): http://usbreastfeeding.org/Issue-Papers/Economics.pdf.

2. Sydney Spiesel, "Tales from the Nursery: The health benefits of breastfeeding may not be what you think," *Slate*, March 27, 2006 (http://www.slatetv.org/id/2138629/).

3. Work can also have an impact on breast-feeding decisions. Economists found that when maternity leave benefits were expanded in Canada, mothers tended to breast-feed, on average, a month longer than prior to the expansion. See Michael Baker and Kevin Milligan, "Maternal Employment, Breastfeeding, and Health: Evidence from Maternity Leave Mandates," *Working Paper*, no. 13188, NBER, June 2007.

4. Stephen Strauss, "Clara M. Davis and the Wisdom of Letting Children Choose Their Own Diets," *Canadian Medical Association Journal* 175, no. 10 (November 7, 2006).

5. This is also the issue with a few other strategies out there. In her book *Deceptively Delicious*, Jessica Seinfeld recommends dressing up good food so that children don't know it's there. But that isn't going

to help children accept healthy food that is naked later on. It seems to me that it will only make them fussier eaters. Another strategy, employed by game theorist Barry Nalebuff, is to give children "veto" rights over three foods that they will never have to eat. Interestingly, his daughter got the raw end of that deal because she didn't realize that zucchini and squash were the same thing (as they are in the United States), and she was upset when she found out. This strategy, while a transparent negotiated outcome, also makes it hard to adjust the price should you need to.

Chapter Five

1. Malcolm Gladwell, "Smaller: The Disposable Diaper and the Meaning of Progress," *The New Yorker*, November 26, 2001, 74–79.
2. Tim Harford, "Undercover Economist: Big Salaries Not So Potty," *Financial Times*, January 12, 2007.
3. Actually, maybe not in Australia but perhaps in the United States; see Hilary Stout, "Family Matters: Hiring Someone Else to Potty-Train Your Kids, Teach Them to Ride a Bike," *Wall Street Journal*, March 31, 2005.

Chapter Six

1. J. Tibballs "Teaching Medical Staff to Handwash," *Medical Journal of Australia* 164 (1996): 395.
2. Stephen J. Dubner and Steven Levitt, "Selling Soap: How Do You Get Doctors to Wash Their Hands?" *New York Times Magazine*, September 24, 2006.
3. Penelope Green, "Saying Yes to Mess," *New York Times*, December 21, 2006.
4. http://delusion.ucdavis.edu/lice.html

Chapter Seven

1. http://www.evolutionshift.com/blog/2006/06/20/a-sweet-story-for-the-future/

Chapter Eight

1. Jay Belsky, Deborah Lowe Vandell, Margaret Burchinal, K. Alison Clarke-Stewart, Kathleen McCartney, and Margaret Tresch Owen, The NICHD Early Child Care Research Network, "Are There Long-Term Effects of Early Child Care?" *Child Development* 78, no. 2 (2007): 681–701.
2. Economists have studied the impact of day care as well. For instance, they have shown that day care has more positive impacts on children when their parents are less educated than when they are highly educated. See David Blau and Janet Currie (2004), "Who's Minding the Kids?: Preschool, Day Care, and After School Care," in *The Handbook of Education Economics*, ed. Finis Welch and Eric Hanushek, vol. 2 (New York: North Holland, forthcoming).
3. "The Kids Are Alright: What the Latest Day-Care Study Really Found," *Slate*, March 28, 2007 (http://www.slate.com/id/2162876).

Chapter Nine

1. More on the AAP's TV guidelines can be found at http://www.aap.org/family/tv1.htm.
2. Matthew Gentzkow and Jesse Shapiro, "Preschool Television Viewing and Adolescent Test Scores: Historical Evidence from the Coleman Study," *Quarterly Journal of Economics* 123, no. 1 (February 2008): 279–323.
3. In a related study, economists have found that television viewing in developing nations can have a positive effect on gender roles. See Robert Jensen and Emily Oster, "The Power of TV: Cable Television and Women's Status in India," mimeo, University of Chicago, Economics, July 30, 2007.
4. Conn Iggulden and Hal Iggulden, *The Dangerous Book for Boys* (London: Collins, 2007).
5. Philip K. Howard, "A Tree Falls in Connecticut," *New York Times*, July 30, 2006.
6. For an interesting account of this, see Emily Bazelon, "Trees versus Children: Are Nut Allergies Taking Over the Planet?" *Slate*, July 27, 2006 (http://slate.com/id/2146628/).

7. Steven D. Levitt, "Evidence that Seat Belts Are as Effective as Child Safety Seats in Preventing Death for Children Aged Two and Up," mimeo, University of Chicago, Economics Department, August 2005.
8. Shirley L. Tonkin, Sally A. Vogel, Laura Bennet, and Alistair Jan Gunn, "Apparently Life Threatening Events in Infant Car Safety Seats," *British Medical Journal* 300 (2006): 1205–1206.

Chapter Ten

1. Emily Bazelon, "Hitting Bottom: Why America should outlaw spanking," Slate, January 25, 2007.

Chapter Eleven

1. Ann Pelo and Kendra Pelojoaquin, "Why We Banned Legos," *Rethinking Schools* 21, no. 2 (Winter 2006).

Chapter Thirteen

1. Deirdre Van Dyk, "$38,000 Kids' Birthday Parties?" *Time*, January 22, 2007.
2. http://www.birthdaypartyideas.com
3. Birthdayswithoutpressure.org.

Chapter Fourteen

1. The classic reference is W. Mischel, Y. Shoda, and M. I. Rodriguez, "Delay of Gratification in Children," *Science* 244, no. 4907 (1989): 933–938. These researchers found that self-control in delaying benefits (in four-year-olds) was correlated with better scholastic performance later on. Of course, such self-control might be a symptom of greater academic ability rather than a cause of it.
2. There are many more stories like the tooth fairy and traffic light episodes at http://www.iusedtobelieve.com.
3. In actuality, Child No. 2 is not alone. It takes some time for children to exhibit patience; this usually occurs by age five. Economists have found that age does, in fact, assist both in patience and in more

rational choices regarding future payoffs. See Eric Bettinger and Robert Slonim, "Patience among children," *Journal of Public Economics* 91 (2007): 343–363.

4. Dweck's study was outlined in Po Bronson, "How (Not) to Talk to Your Kids: The Perverse Power of Praise," *New York Magazine*, February 12, 2007.

5. An enterprising dentist (http://www.decare.com) conducts an annual survey of tooth fairy "per tooth" payments as a barometer of economic activity. In 2007, it was down 15 percent.

Chapter Fifteen

1. "Natural enemies: how to improve the dreaded parent-teacher conference," Slate, February 8, 2007.

Chapter Sixteen

1. Daniel Gilbert, *Stumbling on Happiness* (Boston: Knopf, 2006).

2. Orson Scott Card, "Building better children," *The Rhinoceros Times*, Greensboro, NC, November 16, 2006.

3. Nobel laureate Gary Becker's "Rotten Kid Theorem" demonstrates what caring parents can bring to the world (Gary Becker, *A Treatise on the Family* (Cambridge, MA: Harvard University Press, 1981). It turns out that, if the parent cares about not only their own welfare but also the welfare of their offspring, a child knowing this will not want to ignore their parent's preferences completely when choosing to do something. In effect, that would be biting the hand that feeds them.

Index